High Performance Learning

Schools that want to be world class are now paying attention to the findings from neuroscience and psychology that tell us we can build better brains. They are changing their mindset, expecting success for far more students and no longer being constrained by ideas of genetic potential.

High Performance Learning provides readers with a ground-breaking and approachable model for achieving high levels of academic performance for all students and schools. It takes what is known about how people reach advanced cognitive performance and translates it into a practical and user-friendly framework, which can be used with all students to systematically build the cognitive thinking skills and learner behaviours that will deliver success in school, in the workplace and in later life. Flexible and adaptable, High Performance Learning can be used in any context, with any curriculum and at any age. It does not require separate lessons but rather becomes the underpinning pedagogy of the school.

Drawing on the author's 40 years of research into how the most able students think and learn, this book provides a framework that has been extensively trialled in schools in eleven countries. Themes include:

- Creating world class schools
- The High Performance Learning environment
- The High Performance Learning framework
- Advanced Cognitive Performance characteristics (ACPs)
- Values, Attitudes and Attributes (VAAs)
- Creating and leading a High Performance Learning school
- The role of parents, universities and employers.

This invaluable resource will help schools make the move from good to world class and will be essential reading for school leaders, teachers and those with an interest in outstanding academic performance.

Deborah Eyre is a leading educational writer and influencer in the area of high performance for schools and individuals. She is also an academic, former Education Director at Nord Anglia Education and Director at the UK National Academy for Gifted and Talented Youth (NAGTY).

High Performance Learning

How to become a world class school

Deborah Eyre

Routledge
Taylor & Francis Group

LONDON AND NEW YORK

First published 2016
by Routledge
2 Park Square, Milton Park, Abingdon, Oxon OX14 4RN

and by Routledge
711 Third Avenue, New York, NY 10017

Routledge is an imprint of the Taylor & Francis Group, an informa business

British Library Cataloguing in Publication Data
A catalogue record for this book is available from the British Library

Library of Congress Cataloging in Publication Data
Names: Eyre, Deborah, author.
Title: High performance learning : how to become a world class school /
    Deborah Eyre.
Description: New York, NY : Routledge, 2016. | Includes index.
Identifiers: LCCN 2015026640| ISBN 9781138940116 (hbk) | ISBN
    9781138940130 (pbk) | ISBN 9781315674476 (ebk)
Subjects: LCSH: Cognitive learning. | Thought and thinking—Study and
    teaching. | Learning, Psychology of.
Classification: LCC LB1062.E98 2016 | DDC 371.2/07—dc23
LC record available at http://lccn.loc.gov/2015026640

ISBN: 978-1-138-94011-6 (hbk)
ISBN: 978-1-138-94013-0 (pbk)
ISBN: 978-1-315-67447-6 (ebk)

Typeset in Bembo
by Swales & Willis Ltd, Exeter, Devon, UK

MIX
Paper from
responsible sources
FSC
www.fsc.org   FSC® C013056

Printed and bound in Great Britain by
TJ International Ltd, Padstow, Cornwall

Contents

Illustrations

Figures

Tables

Preface

This book is the culmination of a lifetime's research and practice in education for advanced cognitive performance. It aggregates all I have discovered over the last 40 years of education research and translates it into a practical framework that can easily be adopted for use in school. It builds on the policy paper *Room at the Top: Inclusive Education for High Performance* (London: Policy Exchange, 2010) in which I asserted that high academic performance was an achievable reality for many students, not just the few, and we should accept nothing less.

The ideas in this book are deliberately presented as a framework or scaffold which each school must interpret, rather than a programme to be lifted off the shelf and used in the same way in each school. This is because experience has shown me that each school is a unique institution, and that the best approaches are those that are flexible enough to be bent to fit the individual needs of each school. Also, that deep level change only occurs when teachers and senior leaders engage intensely and genuinely with the central idea and then adapt it to make it their own. Any successful approach must allow the professionals to make adjustments and drive the agenda when it comes to implementation.

My career as a practical academic has included periods when I have worked in academia and focused on research, but it has also included substantial periods when I have been privileged to be part of implementing my new ideas at scale in the educational sphere and evaluating their strengths and weaknesses. This has afforded me the opportunity to work globally with some outstanding education professionals and policy makers, as well as fellow researchers in the field of gifted education. I find myself in awe of what education professionals can achieve and of their creativity. I would like to thank all those, too numerous to mention, whom I have worked with or who have supported my work and been brave enough to disrupt the existing orthodoxies in pursuit of better outcomes for students.

This book is another potential disruption. It lays down the gauntlet for schools and asks them to rethink their expectations completely in the light of new discoveries in neuroscience and psychology. It asks them to set about the task of creating high performers by systematically building better brains. I am absolutely confident that leaders and teachers in good schools across the globe will rise to this challenge and seek to make their schools world class.

I would like to thank Nord Anglia Education for adopting High Performance Learning and being the first to exploit its potential. Also, the truly excellent senior leaders and teachers in the Nord Anglia Education's international schools who brought this to life with outstanding results and showed just what is possible. You know who you are and I am in your debt.

Finally, I would like to thank all my professional colleagues and personal friends – in the UK and overseas – who have offered me ongoing support and encouragement. In particular, I would like to mention my son Richard who shares my love of education and who reads and advises on my work, and Jude, Angharad and John, without whose support this book would never have been produced. Thanks, too, to Kareni Bannister for her keen editorial eye.

Professor Deborah Eyre

Chapter 1

Creating world class schools

World class schools are consistently effective in securing excellent academic results for their students but they also produce students who can think for themselves, are socially confident and have experienced a rich diet of educational opportunities. These students exhibit the characteristics of advanced cognitive performance. At their core, these schools comply with all the features of a well managed organisation and easily meet the requirements set out in any external accountability measures. These external measures are recognised as important building blocks and are not to be underestimated. But world class schools do so much more. They produce consistently large numbers of high achieving students who are college-ready and workplace-ready.

In 2010 in a policy document for Policy Exchange (Eyre, 2010) I suggested that:

> More pupils than we previously thought have the potential to perform at the highest levels – that is to achieve advanced levels of cognitive performance – that the way to secure this is to create a system that expects significantly more from more pupils, and that the consequence of such an approach will be to raise the performance of the whole system, more surely than through any specific structural or pedagogical reform. Gifted education tells us exactly how to achieve this. There really is 'Room at the Top' if we systematically nurture more children to get there.

High Performance Learning is the framework that turns this policy approach into practice. It tells schools 'How to be Top'. It has been proven to work at the 'district level' in Nord Anglia Education's non-selective international schools, where one in five students are now obtaining places in the top thirty universities in the world[1] and these promising outcomes suggest far wider system applicability. High Performance Learning helps individual schools make the move from good to truly world class. It does so by placing student learning and professionalised teachers at the heart of the process and uses a unique, robust and replicable framework at the school level that routinely delivers high performance for the vast majority of students in the school. It systematically teaches students how to be 'intelligent' and how to succeed in school. Furthermore, the students themselves are intellectually and socially confident, workplace-ready and life-ready with a global outlook and a concern for others.

This approach is modern in conception, building on emerging concepts in neuroscience and psychology regarding human potential, on requirements for twenty-first-century employability and societal success and on the known learning patterns of the most advanced or gifted learners. Crucially, High Performance Learning is not a bolt-on programme but rather a lens through which schools can view and develop their own professional practice.

This approach is timely not only for individual schools but also for system reformers. It fits neatly within the post-standardisation paradigm with ambitions that exceed general competence and aim for overall excellence: schools looking to move their performance from 'good' to 'great'. It articulates in detail what that vision should look like at the student level, provides a route map to help individual schools make it a reality and hence has the capacity to move entire education systems as well as schools from good to great. This approach has particular significance for children from low income and disadvantaged backgrounds. These are the students with low aspiration and low intellectual capital. They do not acquire the relevant cognitive and learner skills at home and so stand to benefit disproportionately when they are systematically well taught in school. In essence, High Performance Learning is an evidence-based, practical framework that allows policy makers to devolve ownership for improvement safely to school leaders and teachers, while simultaneously providing a construct that ensures accountability without creating a teach-to-the-test culture in schools. It provides a practical next step in the quest to move on from securing standardisation as a main focus.

It is not the intention in this chapter to review or fully critique the system reform agenda over the past 30 years, but rather to position High Performance Learning within it and to articulate the way in which this very contemporary approach can serve to further the aims of system-wide improvement. It also aims to provide recommendations for ways in which policy makers could support the adoption of the High Performance Learning theory in respect of curriculum, testing, accountability/inspection, teacher quality and funding. This is timely for 'good' systems currently grappling with exactly how to bridge from good to world class.

A brief, simple overview of system reform in the last 30 years

No-one in the education space at any level over the past 30 years can have been untouched by the debates surrounding education policy. When I began teaching in the late 1970s there was no clear definition of what a good school should look like or be trying to achieve. Schools had historically focused mainly on teaching core skills, but some went far beyond that and in a myriad different ways. Truly world class schools such as the top English public (independent) schools were clear about their own individual educational offer and why it was desirable for them, but there was no general consensus for the state-run schools; they varied widely in terms both of quality and approach. Yet in the last 30 years the quest to articulate in detail what constitutes good schools and good education has not only raged but has moved from the dusty corridors of academia to become a matter of political concern and indeed political pride. The debate has also moved from fragmentation to a remarkable degree of consensus. Education has become more standardised.

At the heart of this consensus is agreement that the purpose of schools and schooling is to help students reach levels of educational achievement that will fit them well for future life and feed the demands of an increasingly complex workplace and society. Students being given access to quality schooling until the age of 16+ is now seen as an entitlement – at least in more developed countries. The system has, rightly, become concerned about those groups who do not have access to good quality education and about those individuals and groups who get left behind and do not thrive in their educational setting. This has in turn led to a focus on increasing the number of good schools and reducing the inconsistency of student performance within them.

In their state of the art review of this school effectiveness and school improvement journey Hopkins and colleagues (2014) chart it from its early focus on organisational development to the more recent and familiar areas (Phases 3–5) which have shaped thinking in the last 30 years.

Phase 1 – Understanding the organisational culture of the school.
Phase 2 – Action research and research initiatives at the school level.
Phase 3 – Managing change and comprehensive approaches to school reform.
Phase 4 – Building capacity for student learning at the local level and the continuing emphasis on leadership.
Phase 5 – Towards systemic improvement.

They describe Phase 3 as being characterised by self-managing schools transforming their organisations by managing change in the quest for enhanced student achievement (p. 264) and which gave rise to a series of models of improvement that schools or systems could adopt. Phase 4 enhanced this by focusing on collaboration and networking across groups or districts of schools. It balanced top-down and bottom-up change in order to make measured differences in student achievement (p. 264). Phase 5 shifts the focus to learning about learning and learning from one another.

System improvement strategy over this period has undoubtedly done much to create more consistency in the school system, to the benefit of many students. This has been achieved by setting higher standards for schools and high stakes assessments for students, so ensuring that schools raise their expectations and fewer students fail to achieve the required educational minimums. It has – arguably – set the bar higher and tried to ensure that all institutions and students achieve the minimum standard. It has created a level of coherence and consistency in the international education diaspora and has provided a universal language for education, which assists in both collaborative and comparative work.

It has also, through the work of both the Organisation for Economic Co-operation and Development (OECD) Programme for International Student Assessment (PISA) and McKinsey, challenged assumptions and dispelled myths, for example about the link between spending on education and quality of educational outcomes. It has asked some searching questions as to why schools in cultures as different as Hong Kong and Finland are able to produce consistently good results while others are not. All this debate has helped to give coherence to work on school and system reform. So far, so good.

However, from the outset system reform has exhibited some limitations. Over time these have become more significant and eventually tested achievement reached a plateau (Hargreaves and Shirley, 2008). In the editorial of the anniversary edition of the *Journal of Educational Change*, Hargreaves (2009, p. 258) posed the following question.

Have we seen great breakthroughs and synergies of strategy and impact along with impressive new results? Or have educational reform strategies been just as much a part of the great unraveling of overconfidence and overreach as have the bursting bubbles of speculative investment and uncontrolled indebtedness?

He answers this by suggesting that the journey has been by way of originally large-scale centrally driven approaches that became increasingly prescriptive and demanding, and is now moving towards more developmental approaches as capability in the workforce has increased. He sees this as not just desirable but essential because:

> The ironic effect of international interest in large-scale reform is that it has exposed how the countries and systems that have actually been most successful educationally and economically are ones that provide greater flexibility and innovation in teaching and learning, that invest greater trust in their highly qualified teachers, that value curriculum breadth and that do not try to orchestrate everything tightly from the top.
>
> (2009, p. 13)

Hargreaves is not alone in taking a moment to pause and reframe. Many of the architects of the large-scale system reforms have similarly engaged in a process of determining what to keep and what to ditch as school reform moves to a new stage. Fullan (2009) is somewhat more optimistic. He points to the gains made, including the fact that Singapore, Hong Kong, Finland, Ontario, Alberta and England are all engaged in self-conscious strategy formulation and implementation and looking to see what they can learn from their own and others' experiences and evidence base. But Fullan also sees the need to move on and build capacity in the teaching profession, while continuing a commitment to test-based educational accountability. The period 2008 to 2009 proved to be something of a watershed in terms of school reform.

This centrally driven approach has been successful as a first step and has ratcheted up overall standards in schools. It has seen some notable step-changes in poor performing systems at the district level (London Challenge) but it has not helped systems to reach the world class standards that characterise the very best, nor has it served to meet the needs of the workplace and society. Massachusetts has been one of the most successful systems in terms of reform. Yet in 2014 it recognised that its considerable achievements would still be insufficient for the future. It needed a new transformation (Brightlines, 2014). In framing its future vision it identified six gaps that remained following the first phase.

1   The employability gap: the gap between what the economy demands and what the school system produces.
2   The knowledge gap: the gap between what a twenty-first-century American needs to know and what graduates of the school system actually know.
3   The achievement gap: the gap between Massachusetts students as a whole and those from economically disadvantaged backgrounds.
4   The opportunity gap: the opportunity to succeed between children of the well off and children of low income families.
5   The gap between the performance of Massachusetts and those in the top performing education systems in the world.
6   The top talent gap: the gap between top performing students in Massachusetts and top performing students in the best performing systems in the world.

These gaps are immense in terms of scope and scale. The reasons why this situation has occurred is interesting and important in terms of what that means for current and future system reform. Critics of large-scale target driven system reform in England have suggested that it has led to an increase in schools being deemed 'good' or even 'outstanding' on the school improvement criteria, but it has not resulted in more schools becoming 'world class'. By creating a test-led approach to education, it has created students who are focused on passing the test but have little interest in mastery of the subject and teachers who are similarly focused on passing the inspection test (or other accountability measures) but less interested in creating well rounded, successful students. The methodology has led to an approach whereby government or state knows best and has made teaching a stressful and undesirable profession with excessive workload being one of the top two reasons given for teachers' leaving (Barmby, 2006). In 2013 the OECD figures showed England as having 20 per cent of secondary teachers under the age of 30, the second youngest workforce after Indonesia. This indicates that retention of teachers is a significant issue.

Success has been particularly limited in minority groups, with social mobility stagnating and children from disadvantaged backgrounds much less likely to develop the advanced cognitive skills required to enter a high-status university than their more advantaged peers (fewer than 3 per cent of children from disadvantaged backgrounds in England and the US reached a 'high' standard (Level 5) on the PISA 2009 reading assessment compared with 15 per cent of those from the most advantaged backgrounds). The system continues to fail those who are deemed 'more able' (Ofsted, 2013) and has created school leavers who employers think are not meeting the requirements of the workplace.

These findings are not unique to England and have prompted questions around both the methodology of large-scale reform and the nature of targets or goals by which schools are held to account. Typical questions include the following:

- Is it enough to ask what good schools look like without asking what good education looks like?
- Is schooling just about the ability to pass the exams or should it build a wider, perhaps non-measurable, skills set?
- What kinds of students are these schools producing and do the accountability structures lead to a narrowing of focus regarding the purposes of education and mechanisms for improvement?
- Is this change in attainment levels sustainable or does it merely represent quick wins that satisfy the politicians at the superficial level while simultaneously debasing education?
- Is this one-size-fits-all approach the best way to deal with different contexts and the needs of different groups of students?

These kinds of questions have resulted in the rethinking of system reform generally and in particular are relevant for those who have mastered the first stage and want now to move from good to world class.

System reform post-standardisation

It has become clear that the pathway to 'world class' is a different one from the one to 'good' (Mourshed, Chijioke and Barber, 2010) and that it needs to allow schools greater flexibility to adapt the overall approach to fit their own context and a rethinking of what is of value and importance in education in addition to the core knowledge set. This revised agenda places a greater focus on the teacher and school leaders as opposed to the system as the driver for change and on shaping the teaching profession. This is an agenda that is about moving from central mandating towards a loosening and unleashing of the teaching profession – while still retaining robust accountability mechanisms.

Barber and Mourshed (in McKinsey and Company, 2007) in their initial review of how the top performing systems reach that pinnacle suggested the need for a focus on:

- getting more talented people to become teachers;
- developing these teachers into better instructors;
- ensuring that these instructors deliver consistently for every child in the system.

The post-standardisation agenda recognises that while teachers are crucial, it is not useful to see them simply as technicians in the system. They need to be viewed as real professionals, capable of making judgements about their practice and improving it through self-study, collaboration with others and contribution to the wider professional community. Equally, school leaders need to be able to lead as well as manage their micro-system and to have a relevant vision for their own school, taking into account its unique circumstances. This vision should be located within the system frameworks but finessed to fit the needs of their own context and their own students. So the quality of professional personnel becomes increasingly significant and their engagement in continuing professional development moves from being desirable to being a core essential. This focus on 'professional capital' (Hargreaves and Fullan, 2013) has led to an interest in how the teaching profession can become itself the engine for change and improvement through professional collaboration and debate.

Yet total delegation to schools and teachers without accompanying strong accountability measures risks losing the consistency gains achieved through large-scale system reform. This could result in variability not only in terms of style but also of quality in the system. Some teachers accustomed to responding to centrally driven directions may find it difficult to adjust to the new role allocated to them. So this move at the system level requires some risk management in its approach. In recent years, system reform has begun to focus (Fullan *et al.*, 2015) on the accountability measures within this new framework. It remains the case that core accountability within the educational system relates to student learning and achievement, but there is increasing recognition that learning is not restricted to test scores and may encompass a wider range of values, attitudes and attributes. Some of these are best assessed internally at the school level and consequently this next stage of system reform may place internal accountability ahead of external accountability, with the system merely checking student performance results and post-school destination outcomes while the school determines how best to achieve the required results.

This move towards greater school responsibility is an interesting development because it is starting to reflect the reality of what we know about really good or world class schools. One might say that a major difference between 'good' schools and 'world class' schools is interpretation. In world class schools school leaders and teachers diagnose the needs of their school and customise accepted professional practice, where necessary, for their school, for individuals and subsets of students. Students are also interpreters in this situation and can diagnose their own learning needs and customise the overall offer to suit their own strengths and weaknesses. The collaboration between students and teachers in student learning is more significant. Judgement in all its forms and at all levels is a core skill. The new system reform discussions take a good first step towards recognising the need for teachers to be able to interpret professionally, but this will not be enough on its own. The system developments must also be reflected at the student level in the school's pedagogy. Teachers cannot and should not do this alone. Education is about developing the learners' capabilities and students must play an active role in the process, otherwise they do not become autonomous and independent learners.

Features of world class schools

Throughout the world there are some schools that succeed in producing large numbers of well educated, well rounded students and it is those models we need to understand and emulate. This success does not occur by accident. The schools are well run and managed operationally but they also do much more. In particular, like all good organisations, they have a very clear, aspirational vision and have defined achievable milestones along the journey to achieve it. These cover not only core academic prowess but a wider range of student characteristics such as values and attitudes. World class schools proactively look to address the needs of both minority groups and the individual and they are relentless in the pursuit of success. Each is unique. The schools provide a glittering array of imaginative learning opportunities designed to fit their particular context, the needs of their learners and of their community. They deliberately draw on the strengths of the staff team and the heritage of the school. There is a palpable sense of purpose and excitement in each one and both students and staff enjoy the schooling experience.

Most crucially, world class schools place the learners at the heart of the enterprise and build the supporting frameworks around them. This means that pedagogy takes precedence, with supporting systems and structures enabling pedagogy as opposed to defining it. Teachers play a central role as the major enablers of effective pedagogy. They constitute a professionalised workforce, working collaboratively from an evidential base and combining research and practice to propel improvements through the use of increasingly effective pedagogies. The principals and senior leaders are the guardians of the educational vision; they ensure that management is effective but does not detract from the school's more ambitious goals. Data are used to measure progress against the vision, but it is acknowledged that not everything can or should be measured. Students and staff at all levels feel an emotional attachment to the school and this is also reflected in parental feedback.

Central to the mission of world class schools is excellent academic performance. High achievement at school is recognised as the foundation for lifetime success. World class schools are scholarly places where everyone – students, teachers, support staff and visitors – is looking to maximise learning outcomes for students and to remove barriers that prevent some students from achieving. Learning is genuinely and highly valued and this is evident. Teachers talk about what they are reading or learning, and so do students – often with each other.

But academic success is not defined merely as the ability to pass the test. World class schools are not test-passing factories. They focus on a more creative rounded view of learning, emphasising the rewards of deep understanding and mastery of the subject. They are developing learner capability and nurturing a love of learning and its challenges. This implies the development of autonomy and confidence in the learner as well as the motivation to succeed. Students in world class schools want to learn and find that the school appreciates their efforts. They develop not only academic competence but also the values, attitudes and attributes that will serve them well in university, the workplace and their life.

Interestingly, world class schools have often been frustrated by the large-scale system reform agenda which they see as narrow and unimaginative. They want more demanding targets. World class schools start with their vision. As in all successful organisations this drives their progress but, as with other organisations, the nature of that vision is vital. Under the large-scale system reform agenda school visions have sometimes tended to become narrow and short term. They focus on improvements that will secure wins in the short term, such as better inspection outcomes next time around, rather than projecting into the longer term. The school may also have a mission statement which is more aspirational, but it is generally not connected to measurable action. Creating a strong vision built around the profile of the student the school seeks to produce helps to frame and drive all of the subsequent direction of travel. As in all successful organisations this clear sense of purpose is vital to securing success.

World class schools exhibit all the characteristics of good schools, but they are truly student centred and have some additional features that make the difference (see Table 1.1).

The role of High Performance Learning

It is the case that currently only a minority of schools manage to steer themselves to achieving world class. If the system is to produce more of these schools, then some leadership and guidance around the journey will be needed to accelerate the speed of development. This system guidance should reflect the post-standardisation agenda of building on professional capital, but it should go further in terms of helping the profession itself to move forward and not wait for schools and groups of schools to invent their own wheel. The system needs to set expectations, not regarding what a world class school should look like in terms of systems and processes, but rather what such a school should expect to deliver for its students. An outcome-based accountability structure. Accountability

Table 1.1 Features of world class schools

1	They start by focusing on the profile of the type of student they want to develop and build their accountability measures around this.
2	They select a core curriculum that is overall well suited to their vision and then audit it in order to enhance and supplement where needed, including via the enrichment offer.
3	They make explicit to students (and parents) what they are trying to achieve and how they should participate.
4	They are confident on behalf of their students, who feel they can trust the school to help them be successful.
5	They see personal and pastoral support and guidance as crucial to academic success.
6	They see the school as a well oiled machine that can deliver the same high standards for students year on year and regardless of background.
7	They are purposeful but also relaxed, with both students and staff at ease in the school.
8	They place a high level of trust in their teachers and their students and structures assume timely intervention and benchmarking rather than constant monitoring.
9	Internal accountability precedes external accountability and they take ownership for their own performance.
10	Everyone feels an emotional attachment to the school but they don't see themselves as world class because they are never complacent and are continually seeking to refine and improve.

systems should be predicated on the basis that internal accountability within the school is the primary driver of quality and can dictate methodology, while external accountability provides public reassurance and should require a light touch and rest on a principle of intervention in inverse proportion to success.

The world's top schools have always focused firmly on helping their students reach not only high exam scores but the wider concept of advanced cognitive performance. It is more important now than it has ever been for all schools to secure this for as many students as possible. In an increasingly global and competitive world a happy and secure future cannot be taken for granted. At the national level, economic success is predicated on us finding and nurturing talent for the common good (Eyre, 2009b). In England, the current generation is poorer than the previous one and this is the first time in the developed world that personal wealth has plateaued or indeed reversed. Good academic qualifications at school and university level also place the individual at an advantage and that in turn creates power and choice. Alison Woolf (2002, p. 244) describes this as follows.

> The lesson of the last century must be that, for individuals, it (education) matters more than ever before in history. And not just any education: the right qualifications, in the right subjects, from the right institutions, is of ever-growing importance.

High performance for the many, not the few

Educational orthodoxies in the past have held that this nirvana is desirable but inevitably limited to a minority of schools and students. This should no longer be the case. We now know from work done in neuroscience that the brain is malleable (Jonides *et al.*, 2012) and that, in theory at least, students are capable of becoming more intelligent and achieving the academic results that were once the domain of the few. Similarly, as we have learned more about the nature of giftedness and about 'gifted' people, leading research has shifted away from identifying cohorts of gifted students and towards creating the educational conditions in which 'giftedness' might best be developed – the 'Human Capital' paradigm (Eyre, 2009b). These types of changes are not yet well recognised or understood by policy makers, who continue to think that each of us possesses a set measure of inherited cognitive ability that will determine our finite performance level. This is outdated and incorrect and limits conceptions of what an education system can deliver. In system reform we need to reflect the emerging knowledge as opposed to historic understandings.

The creation of High Performance Learning for the many is what the system should expect from schools. We must move away from schools seeing themselves as having 'good' or 'poor' cohorts academically but instead focus on students in a school, almost all of whom are capable of significant academic success. While recognising that the journey will be more difficult for some than others, the goal of a world class school is to become increasingly efficient at making academic success a reality for more of its students year on year.

What the system should expect is that every year and in every school significant numbers of students will be reaching high levels of academic performance and that year on year schools will become increasingly proficient at delivering this result.

A school vision based on a student profile of work-ready and life-ready students

High Performance Learning helps schools to deliberately and systematically develop both the cognitive skills needed for academic success in school and the wider set of set of skills that are needed for lifetime success. One of the features of world class schools is that they do not teach to the test, but rather they develop the broader range of cognitive skills and in addition develop the values, attitudes and attributes that are critical to helping students achieve good academic outcomes and make them college-ready, employment-ready and indeed life-ready. World class schools have broader horizons and see the whole learning journey as opposed to sharp segmentation, which leads to teaching to the next test. This approach has been found to be significant in securing success both in school and post-school as students are not merely competent but also motivated and inventive.

Cognitive and learner skills need to be at the core, made explicit and developed systematically over the entire duration of schooling as opposed to cognitive skills being implicit in lessons and learner skills introduced as soft skills or employability skills when the student is close to leaving school. The High Performance Learning framework sets out progress routes for twenty generic characteristics students need to develop if they are to be more successful in cognitive domains and ten values, attitudes and attributes that develop the wider learner dispositions needed for lifetime success. These can help to provide a framework for development while enabling schools to customise to fit their vision and curriculum.

An appropriate and demanding curriculum

World class schools develop these cognitive skills and learner dispositions through their approach to pedagogy. Their curriculum and assessment systems are constructed to develop these skills and dispositions just as surely as they aim to acquire subject and cross-curricular knowledge. The core curriculum at the system level should therefore be as routinely demanding as it is in the world's top performing systems. High levels of subject knowledge and skills characterise the top performers on the Programme for International Student Assessment (PISA)[2] tests and should be the mark of any curriculum, but the choice of knowledge needs to be a mix of that which is enduring and has been a part of school curriculum over time and that which is new and pertinent. This is particularly so in the STEM (Science, Technology, Engineering and Maths) subjects, but is also evident in the arts subjects where the global nature of the modern world makes a parochial curriculum a limitation in terms of future employability and contribution to society.

The system debate around knowledge versus the use and application of knowledge sets a challenge for policy makers. A skills-based competency curriculum is optimal for building the learner capabilities of individuals, while subject-based curricula sequence the acquisition of cognitive knowledge and skills. Neither is better than the other.

What is clear is that the best schools are reaching for high educational standards and use a demanding curriculum as the backdrop. They build the performance of students through access to a diverse, interesting and demanding set of learning opportunities that enable students to practise and hone these skills. They then construct their formative assessment frameworks around the curriculum and it is success in these, for increasing numbers of individuals, that leads to system success. Some of these opportunities are in core lessons but others arise through competitions, community service, extra-curricular clubs, inter-school activities and collaboration of students at the regional, national and global levels. The high performance expectations can be applied to any curriculum but the more demanding and relevant the curriculum the easier it is for the school to succeed.

Recommendation 3

School – Curricula should be demanding, contemporary and relevant. The definition of curriculum should recognise the multiple and varied contexts in which learning may occur face to face and online.

System – The system should set out expectations that are demanding, contemporary and relevant. The extent to which these are prescribed is dependent on national context, but it should go without saying that if the system wants to create world class schools it should not attempt to micro-manage classroom delivery through the curriculum.

High performance for all socio-economic and ethnic groups

A significant barrier to achieving high performance for the majority of students is the compelling evidence of underperformance and lack of opportunity among disadvantaged and low income groups. This is not a universal issue but it is a systemic problem in some countries, including the USA and England. PISA results show that children from similar social backgrounds can demonstrate very different performance levels, depending on the school they go to or the country they live in. The 10 per cent most disadvantaged 15-year-olds in Shanghai have better maths skills than the 10 per cent most privileged students in the United States and several European countries. In England the family into which you were born is the strongest predictor of how well you will do in school.

This discrepancy is most pronounced where systems incorporate a high degree of stratification. According to the OECD (Schleicher, 2015) none of the countries with a high degree of stratification, whether in the form of tracking, streaming, or grade repetition, is among the top performing education systems or among the systems with the highest share of top performers. This is unsurprising because in a stratified system there are inevitably winners and losers. In England and the USA the losers are usually those from disadvantaged backgrounds. They start school having had limited opportunities and consequently underperform in their early years. They then enter a system where performance in tests steers them into ability groups at an increasingly early age with lower expectations for lower groups. This ensures that those in lower groups will never catch up. The system causes them to underperform in the long term. The minority who do well are succeeding against the odds and in this instance school is compounding rather than mitigating disadvantage.

Some systems are moving away from one in which students are streamed into different types of secondary schools (OECD, 2012). Those countries did not accomplish the transition by taking the average and setting the new standards according to that level. Instead, they levelled up, requiring all students to meet the standards that they had formerly expected only their elite students to meet. This is what the system overall needs to expect, but it will accelerate the process if schools are helped to know how to work in this way.

Recommendation 4

School – Schools should ensure that students from low incomes families and disadvantaged groups have access to the same demanding opportunities as other students and can rely on the support needed to help them succeed. Students' grouping arrangements generally must not disadvantage students who are slower to achieve high performance.

System – However the system is organised, it should be unequivocal in respect of its recommendations of high performance and continue to drive proactively for equity for disadvantaged groups.

High performing teachers and school leaders create high performing students

High performance for the many requires a high-quality teaching force. World class schools depend on their teachers to deliver the required outcomes and it is only in a system in which teachers see themselves as professionals and take responsibility for their own work that world class schools can exist. Collaboration within and across schools has been shown to be the best way to improve teaching quality and develop greater levels of consistent quality within good schools that are looking to get even better. Innovation tends to come from the bottom up in these schools as well as from the top down. Teachers take responsibility for their own professional development and see it as a daily aspect of their professional practice as well as an episodic event when formal learning occurs. They tinker with their practice in order to develop it rather than making large switches from one approach to another.

School leaders occupy the key accountability role and hold the responsibility for the health of their school. In world class schools senior leaders embrace this responsibility and are confident about the direction of travel, and the strengths and weaknesses of the school, departments, systems and processes and of individuals. They work collaboratively to develop consistency of overall approach and of standards. There is a no blame culture in the school but instead an emphasis on improving and solving problems. High Performance Learning provides a rubric to assist in this endeavour while enabling maximum flexibility for interpretation.

Recommendation 5

School – Teachers and school leaders must take ownership for continuous improvement in their school and their practice.

System – The system should ensure a supply of high-quality teachers, counsellors and classroom assistants, etc. and should promote high-quality school leadership at all levels.

Summary

What must change in the system is that schools must produce the types of students that the workplace and society need, and it must produce them in large numbers. We have to be just as deliberate, systematic and relentless in this pedagogical quest as we were in creating large-scale school reform. We must give greater precedence to internal accountability and allow the school and its professionals to be the driver for change while maintaining light touch external accountability.

The High Performance Learning framework provides schools with an underpinning philosophy that can help them to make this a reality and a systematic framework to steer their progress. It draws on the body of research evidence into how the most able students come to succeed academically and translates it into a pedagogical framework that can be used to create a student-focused vision of institutional success and the mechanisms for making high academic achievement the outcome for most or all students. In this policy approach a focus on the student is the vehicle for moving the system from good to excellent.

Notes

1 QS rankings.
2 Programme for International Student Assessment. Available online at http://www.oecd.org/pisa/aboutpisa.

References

Barber, M. and Mourshed, M. (2007). *How the World's Best-performing Schools Come Out on Top*. London: McKinsey & Company.

Barmby, P. W. (2006). Improving teacher recruitment and retention: The importance of workload and pupil behaviour. *Educational Research*, 48(3), 247–265.

Brightlines (2014). *The New Opportunity to Lead: A Vision for Education in Massachusetts in the Next 20 Years*. Available at: http://www.mbae.org/wp-content/uploads/2014/03/New-Opportunity-to-Lead.pdf.

Eyre, D. (2009a). The English model of gifted education. In L. V. Shavinina (ed.), *The International Handbook on Giftedness*. New York: Springer, pp. 1045–1059. doi: org/ 10.1007/978-1-4020-6162-2_53.

Eyre, D. (ed.) (2009b). *Major Themes in Gifted and Talented Education* (4 volumes). London: Routledge.

Eyre, D. (2010). *Room at the Top: Inclusive Education for High Performance*. London: Policy Exchange.

Fullan, M. (2009). Large-scale reform comes of age. *Journal of Educational Change*, 10(2–3), 101–113.

Fullan, M., Rincón-Gallardo, S. and Hargreaves, A. (2015). Professional capital as accountability. *Education Policy Analysis Archives*, 23(14–17), 1–18. doi:10.14507/epaa.v23.1998.

Hargreaves, A. (2009). A decade of educational change and a defining moment of opportunity – an introduction. *Journal of Educational Change*, 10(2/3), 89–100. doi:10.1007/s10833-009-9103-4

Hargreaves, A. and Fullan, A. (2013). The power of professional capital: With an investment in collaboration, teachers become nation builders. *Forward Learning*, 34(3). Available at: http://www.forward-learning.org.

Hargreaves, A. and Shirley, D. (2008). Beyond standardization: Powerful new principles for improvement. *Phi Delta Kappan*, 90(2), 135–143.

Hopkins, D., Stringfield, A., Harris, A., Stoll, L. and Mackay, T. (2014). School and system improvement: A narrative state-of-the-art review. *School Effectiveness and School Improvement: An International Journal of Research, Policy and Practice*, 25(2), 257–281. doi:10.1080/09243453.2014.885452.

Jonides, J., Jaeggi, S. M., Buschkuehl, M. and Shah, P. (2012). Building better brains. *Scientific American Mind*, 23(4), 59–63.

Mourshed, M., Chijioke, C. and Barber, M. (2010). *How the World's Most Improved School Systems Keep Getting Better*. London: McKinsey & Company.

OECD (2012). *PISA Results: What Makes Schools Successful? Resources, Policies and Practices (Volume IV)*. Available at: http://www.oecd.org/pisa/keyfindings/pisa-2012-results-volume-iv.htm.

Ofsted (2013). *The Most Able Students: Are They Doing as Well as They Should in Our Non-selective Secondary Schools?* (130118). Available at: http:// www.gov.uk/government/publications/are-the-most-able-students-doing-as-well-as-they-should-in-our-secondary-schools.

Schleicher, A. (2015). Seven big myths about top-performing school systems. *BBC News*, 4 February 2015. Available at: http://www.bbc.co.uk/news/business-31087545.

Woolf, A. (2002). *Does Education Matter?* London: Penguin Books.

Chapter 2

The High Performance Learning environment

As established in the previous chapter, good schools become great schools not by applying the same teaching methodologies that have helped them reach 'good', but rather by doing something different. What I suggest in this chapter is indeed different, but it is also evidence-based, logical and practical and leads to great outcomes. It requires the school to start by thinking about the student rather than the structure, because when it comes to schooling what every parent wants is for their child to succeed educationally. Indeed, what every school wants is for its students to achieve highly and what every education system wants is to produce a highly educated workforce. The role of the school is to make that a reality.

High Performance Learning is an advanced pedagogy that helps schools to become world class through systematically developing superior cognitive performance in all students. It enables students to enhance and build their own ability and to use it productively to obtain good academic results. It is evidence based, using the latest research in psychology and neuroscience. It does not provide a guarantee that every single student will eventually attain high performance, but many more will do so and this approach gives students the very best possible chance of success. And, in doing so, they will not only perform well academically but also develop the values, attitudes and attributes that equip them for success in life beyond school. In world class schools the number of students achieving highly will grow year on year as the school becomes more proficient. High Performance Learning actively avoids labelling students as 'less able' or 'more able', but instead sees high academic performance as learnable and focuses on unleashing the learning ability we all possess and systematically developing it into an advanced form.

High Performance Learning differs from existing practices in four ways.

1   It assumes that high performance for most is a possible outcome.
2   It systematically builds the skills that enable high performance and creates schools with many high performing students – regardless of their performance on entry.
3   It expects schools to become increasingly proficient in obtaining this outcome for their students and this is their key accountability measure.
4   It depends on a professionalised teaching force using their professional capital to achieve this.

Setting the new education stage

In adopting a High Performance Learning approach schools need to learn from the research about how people get to be successful in life and what makes the difference between success and failure. This enables the school to be more systematic in securing success for more individuals and less likely to waste talent. It is only when a school is able to deliver cognitive success *routinely* for the vast majority of its students and, moreover, ensure they are responsible, caring, confident and enterprising, that it can be considered a world class school.

> Delivering success . . . is not like entering your numbers into a lottery. You cannot rely on chance to deliver success; if you do, you are as likely to be successful as you are at winning the lottery. Accompanied by hard work, the delivery of success is wholly reliant on a carefully and meticulously structured process. Remember the best way to predict success is to create it.
>
> (Whyte, 2015, p. 37)

While there is no single route to high achievement, there are some factors which are important generally and some which are specific to school-aged students.

In very simple terms we know the following.

- It is a bumpy road for everyone. No-one achieves highly without meeting obstacles that have to be overcome.
- Success in any field requires a combination of domain skills and cognitive ability.
- Each generation is operating in a more sophisticated context than the previous one, and successful individuals are those who are able to exploit this.
- Each individual needs support, but in the end it is his or her own personal journey and he or she must want to do well.
- Successful people celebrate and enjoy each step of the journey and recognise what they have achieved.

In school, these factors should help to guide us both in what we provide for students and in what we say to students about their journey to success. A useful way to approach this is to focus on potential, opportunities, support and motivation (see Figure 2.1).

Think differently about 'potential'

It is almost certainly the case that the education world itself ensures that schools are unlikely to deliver academic success for all students because it believes that this is simply not possible. High Performance Learning is different. It assumes that most students are capable of performing highly. They are not restricted by having inherited a certain fixed level of ability. Traditionally, teachers are trained to assume that children are born with a finite level of ability and that the role of the school is to help that student to fulfil his or her potential – however great or minor that might be. The numbers for whom academic success can be fully realised are consequently restricted because some students are just inherently more able than others and there is little a school – or parents – can do to change this. Good schools and caring parents have always sought to maximise that

The formula

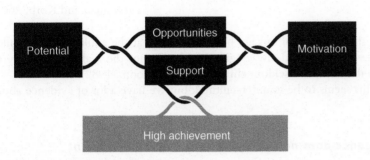

Figure 2.1 The High Performance Learning formula

Source: Eyre (2007).

individual potential, but they have largely accepted that high levels of educational performance will always be for the minority of students rather than the majority. That's just the way it is.

So, instead of aiming high for everyone, education has committed to becoming more and more adept in measuring how much cognitive potential each child possesses and using tests to define this. On the basis of the results we make confident predictions from an increasingly early age about who will do well and exactly how well we expect them to do. Schools doing particularly well are said to add more value, but this is still only adding value to a fixed ability level. While we are all familiar with the nature versus nurture arguments and have accepted that environmental contexts, family background, and so on, can play a part, we stay wedded to the idea that these are less important than inherited characteristics. We still persist in thinking that in the end it is all in the genes.

This is holding us back. High Performance Learning is based on the 'Human Capital' paradigm, which suggests that notions of fixed ability are flawed and outdated. All or most students are capable of achieving highly. We can learn how to exploit, or manage, any inherited predispositions and make ourselves successful.

The evidence in support of this change in mindset is comprehensive and wide-ranging. It comes from the fields of education, neuroscience and psychology.

Once-gifted-always-gifted turns out not to be the reality

It tends to be assumed that children who start out ahead of others will remain high achievers. Of course some late developers may take a while to get moving, but generally it is assumed that the child's position at the start of school is merely amplified as school progresses. Certainly by the time a child moves from primary (elementary) to secondary (high) school it is assumed that the die is cast.

In fact, this is not the case. The students who can be said to be performing best across the lifetime of compulsory schooling vary. A child could be well ahead of his or her peers at age 7 and merely be keeping pace by 17 or could be behind at age 7 and a top performer at 17. These are shifting sands.

When cohorts of children are tested at a young age plus regularly retested over time, the scores show substantial year-to-year regression, disproving the common myth that a child considered gifted at aged six would still be considered gifted at 16.

(Lohman and Korb, 2006)

The evidence also shows a lack of linkage between success at the adult level and childhood precociousness. Once-gifted-always-gifted is simply not the reality: 'Contrary to popular belief, gifted adults were seldom child prodigies' (Bloom, 1982).

At first glance this seems to be counter-cultural, but we have a lot of evidence about why this is so.

Inherited intelligence does not always lead to high achievement

It is the case that some people seem to be born with inherited predispositions that enable them to demonstrate early progress in cognitive domains and it was first assumed that this would predict eventual adult success.

Very early thinkers, such as Louis Terman (1925), assumed that intelligence would inevitably lead to achievement but discovered that these two factors were 'far from perfectly correlated'. Terman is famous for his lifetime study of 1,470 students selected from a possible cohort of 250,000 in California on the basis of an ability test.[1] He began work in 1921 and his subjects were researched throughout their entire lifetimes. He expected that they would go on to be the big thinkers of their age, but in fact most were relatively successful but unremarkable and some failed to achieve at all. By contrast, two children who were tested but rejected, William Shockley and Luis Alvarez, went on to win Nobel Prizes. So exceptional intelligence, as tested, was – perhaps surprisingly – not a particularly strong component of high performance.

What does lead to high achievement?

Arguments have raged throughout the twentieth century about which markers would in fact predict success. From Guilford's (1967) ideas on creativity to Sternberg's ideas on wisdom (Sternberg, 2010), all suggest that ability, as we usually understand it, is not just something theoretical but rather a dynamic concept that requires the facility to apply understanding and ideas as well as just have them. This means that a wholly passive education experience will not help students to develop this dynamism and thus realise their academic prowess.

When this same quest for markers is applied retrospectively to the childhoods of successful adults (Bloom, 1982), some character and personality characteristics emerge as significant and in cognitive attainment. These include willingness to work, competitiveness and the ability to learn rapidly. For example, in maths, curiosity and question-asking coupled with the ability to think and reflect independently have been influential in securing high levels of performance. So it is not just the ability to think at a higher level, but also about how an individual behaves as a learner that counts.

What emerges from all this work is that there is a basket of non-genetic factors that make a really significant difference and that these are already identified and understood in the research literature and can be applied systematically in the education system to enable more students to achieve high performance.

We have seen that people can fail at school and go on to take academic degrees

Of course not all students have traditionally succeeded at school. A good example of late academic achievement is success at university where the academic standards are high. The UK's prestigious Open University, arguably one of England's greatest educational success stories, has an open entry policy. Students' previous academic achievements are not taken into account for entry to most undergraduate courses and many students have only limited formal qualifications: 'Right from the start it adopted a radical open admissions policy, while attaining the highest standards of scholarship. It was a model which proved extremely popular with the public' (Open University, 2015).

In 1969, when the idea of the Open University was announced, it was described as 'blithering nonsense' by Iain Macleod MP, and he was expressing the thoughts of many. How could a real university cater for people who had failed to achieve in school? If they were university material, then they would surely have the necessary qualifications. But half a century later we know that those without conventional qualifications can go on to achieve very highly indeed, and by 2013 the OU was educating 200,000 students, and many other universities had similarly introduced their own access courses. Lack of success at school does not mean lack of ability.

The changing performance of minority or disadvantaged groups

Similarly, there was a time when it was thought that girls did not possess the same intellectual powers as boys. They were thought to be unable to tackle the more academic subjects. It was needlework and domestic science for girls and Latin and physics for boys. Life has certainly proved that girls are quite capable of dealing with the most demanding subjects, and not just a few girls. They are currently outperforming boys at every level in most developing countries and in all phases of schooling in the UK.[2] In January 2014 there were 580,000 applications for places at British higher education institutions. Of these, 333,700 were women, almost 58 per cent of all applicants. In the 2013 GCSE results 24.8 per cent of exams sat by girls were graded A* or A, compared with just 17.6 per cent of those taken by boys. And the story is the same for every age group.

Underachievers who just didn't 'get' school

Even at the individual level we know that some high performers were not conventional high achievers at school. Professor Angie Hobbs, Professor of Public Understanding of Philosophy at the University of Sheffield, when discussing her schooling in an interview for the BBC Radio 4 programme *Desert Island Discs* (BBC Radio, 2015), says that she: 'Wasn't the kind of student they wanted. Didn't get it. Never seeking to be naughty but always getting into trouble.'

What can we conclude about these people who did not always thrive in school but who went on in later life to perform highly? Well, first, they exist in large numbers; these are not just a small minority of underachievers. Second, the reasons that they did not achieve vary and encompass a whole range from home background to school expectations, but crucially it is rarely the result of lack of innate ability.

The brain is more malleable than we thought

The major finding that helps us to understand all this comes from neuroscience. In short, the brain is more malleable than we thought (Jaeggi *et al.*, 2008). It has been known for some time that performance on simple trained tasks can be dramatically improved through practice. However, the more important fluid intelligence (Gf), the ability to reason and to solve new problems independently of previously acquired knowledge, was not previously considered trainable. This fluid intelligence is crucial for effective learning and it has previously been assumed that it was an inherited characteristic. It has now been shown that it is trainable, and this means we can not only learn knowledge but also the more advanced aspects of intelligence. Equally, the brain adapts to its context (Greenfield, 2014, p. xi). If we create the optimal learning opportunities and challenge students, their brains will adjust. We can build better brains and help students to become more intelligent.

We need to believe this, let go of old practices that suggest limits on learning capability and dispel the fears that stop us embracing the idea of achieving the impossible.

Summary

In reality, it turns out that when you ensure that students have the right opportunities, the right support and a belief that they can achieve highly, then most of them do. Lack of innate ability is not the primary reason for failing to reach high academic standards. More significant reasons statistically are related to gender expectations, socio-economic background, cultural traditions and specific learning difficulties. All these are barriers that can be addressed.

So in High Performance Learning we see all students as potentially capable of high academic performance and we enhance the chances of their succeeding by removing individual barriers and actively teaching them how to be intelligent. We do not make assumptions based on ability and we do not segregate children based on their perceived academic ability and hence limit their chances of academic success. Instead of segregating and creating different pathways for different students, we need to help every student follow the route to high academic performance because this gives them maximum options in later life. It is no longer acceptable to talk about 'more able' or 'less able' students.

The first step towards progress in High Performance Learning is the shift in mindset towards expecting all students to be able to achieve highly. Of course, for some, the route is more complex than for others and may take longer, but it is just as achievable – at least in theory. As in learning to drive, some will show a ready aptitude and others will take longer to master the skill and pass the test – but that does not indicate how good their driving will be in the long term.

A useful way to summarise why intelligence is – refreshingly – more complex than at first thought is through Sternberg's description (Henshon, 2008) of his WICS theory.

> People can be smart in three different ways: analytically (as measured by conventional ability tests), creatively, and practically. People are successfully intelligent to the extent that they capitalize on their strengths in these areas and correct or compensate for their weaknesses. I developed the theory by observing students, and in

particular, three of them. Alice was a student who was very high in standardized tests but tended not to be very creative. She was very good at remembering things and analyzing things, but she wasn't very good at coming up with her own ideas. I realized from her that someone could have a very high IQ and high test scores, in general, but not be creative. Another student, Barbara, was very creative but had low test scores and she was initially rejected by Yale's graduate program in psychology. I hired her and she proved to be extremely creative. She showed us that some very creative people don't test well. She was very imaginative but it didn't show up in tests. The problem is that most creative people who don't test well never get a chance to succeed because our society is so test-crazy. A third student, Celia, wasn't all that analytical or creative but she got every job she applied for; what she had was very high practical intelligence. She could go into a job interview, figure out what people wanted to hear, and give it to them. Thus, some people succeeded by virtue of their practical and interpersonal skills. The last thing I have added to the theory, now called WICS (wisdom-intelligence-creativity-synthesized), is wisdom. The importance of wisdom became clear to me in looking at failed leaders. There are really smart people who are unwise.

(Henshon, 2008, p. 77)

Raise the bar and give students a regular diet of advanced learning opportunities so that they can practise and improve

However, a change in mindset alone will not deliver the required result of far more students reaching high levels of performance. It will help but it is not enough. We need to plan proactively for success and build capability – and systematically teach people how to be more intelligent. We need to make success the goal and set about removing the institutional barriers that stop individuals from reaching it. What is needed is a detailed, deliberate and systematic approach.

It is certainly the case that levels of opportunity make an immense difference to whether or not someone can learn how to achieve in a given domain, and so opportunity is probably the most influential factor on the road to success. This is why good schools produce greater numbers of achieving students. They offer better and more advanced learning opportunities. If we want high performance for the many, the step-change has to be that we make advanced learning opportunities available widely and not just for the few. All students need deliberately and regularly to be exposed, from an early age, to opportunities to develop and practise advanced ways of thinking and learner behaviours because it is these that are the key to academic success.

The High Performance Learning framework provides the way to create a systematic approach to the creation of opportunities. It takes what we now know about the characteristics of advanced cognitive performance and translates it into a practical and user-friendly framework that can be used with all students and staff; flexible and adaptable enough to be used in any context, with any curriculum and at any age; not requiring separate lessons, but rather constituting the underpinning pedagogy or 'DNA' of the school. It shows schools how to create advanced learning opportunities and tells students what skills they need to develop.

Who should have access to the advanced learning opportunities and why?

Most teachers know how to create advanced learning opportunities but make them available only to the most able. Creating advanced learning opportunities is not as difficult as it sounds. When I first began working on how to challenge the most able students in the ordinary classroom (Eyre, 1997), I became fascinated by the techniques that could be used to generate greater levels of challenge for the most able. These enquiry-based techniques were innovative, engaging for students (and teachers) and created autonomous and confident learners. Yet from the outset I was troubled by the practical question of who in the class should be the beneficiaries of these more demanding tasks. It seemed to me that they were the optimal learning opportunities and so ideally everyone should have access to them, although some students would be more obvious candidates. Yet this was not the accepted wisdom. They were a diet only suitable for the most able (gifted) students.

Over time, my interest in this type of advanced learning as a form of educational provision increased and moved from looking at existing models and tasks towards the underpinning learning theories that dictate conceptions of advanced cognitive performance and how best to build education around this destination. But the question of who should receive this diet remained unresolved. It definitely worked well with cohorts of identified gifted students, but it also worked well with a wider group. Over time, other teachers working on gifted education have also found this to be the case.

> Where teachers have focused on planning to create challenge for the most able/gifted pupils, they often then choose to make the task available to a wider group of children, sometimes offering additional support to allow other pupils to access the same task. Reasons given for this by teachers in the Oxfordshire Primary Teacher Research Network are both pragmatic and pedagogical. In terms of classroom management a reduction in the number of tasks on offer allows for smoother operation and time for the teacher to work with individuals. In pedagogical terms the challenging tasks require more 'expert behaviour' or 'higher order thinking' and lead to higher levels of attainment but are also intellectually stimulating and likely to be highly motivating regardless of a child's ability level.
>
> (Eyre and McClure, 2001, p. 18)

In 2008 I explored this question more fully while undertaking a review of the field of gifted education over the last 50 years (Eyre, 2009b). What emerged was a set of facts that added real weight to the idea that we should not be trying to find the 'gifted', but instead be looking to create them through the systematic use of advanced learning techniques. What 50 years of research indicates is as follows.

- Over the last century definitions of ability and intelligence have fragmented and there is no longer universal consensus regarding the characteristics of either.
- Hence, identification systems of any kind aimed at creating cohorts of more able/gifted students are inherently unstable.
- Neuroscience is demonstrating that the brain is malleable and can be trained to perform better cognitively.

- Selected cohorts of gifted students across the world show bias against minority, disadvantaged groups.
- Control groups perform as well as identified 'gifted' students on advanced learning opportunities when given the same opportunities.
- Enrichment programmes can raise aspirations and give initial exposure to advanced learning but cannot compensate for poor quality schooling, especially in the case of the disadvantaged.
- The advanced performance of gifted cohorts is largely a result of ongoing access to superior learning opportunities.
- For any students – those selected onto a gifted cohort or otherwise – advanced performance is the result of deliberate, frequent and regular practice of advanced thinking skills coupled with appropriate learner behaviours, e.g. values, attitudes and attributes.

What do we mean by advanced learning opportunities?

When you think about high or advanced cognitive performance you should not confuse it with traditional approaches that 'teach to the test'. Although good test scores will be an obvious outcome, advanced cognitive performance is a more holistic idea. It involves the ability to think flexibly and creatively and to self-regulate when an initial idea doesn't work (Shore, 2000). That doesn't mean that learning time-honoured facts and knowledge is unimportant, but rather that it is insufficient. You need to have a store of interconnected knowledge if you are to think flexibly and creatively. In fact, helping young children make connections in their factual learning is an important preliminary step on the road to high performance.

Advanced learning opportunities tend to focus on critical and creative thinking and on problem-solving. They may use more difficult texts or work with complex ideas and they will be challenging for the individual. They may be extended in duration in order to allow for depth, or pacy in order to require rapid decision-making. They may introduce technical language or domain-specific skills and techniques. But although they are demanding, they should also be enjoyable and interesting so as to stimulate curiosity and motivation. The High Performance Advanced Cognitive Performance characteristics (ACPs) and Values, Attitudes and Attributes (VAAs) provide a structure or rubric for creating advanced learning tasks.

Creating these kinds of opportunities is also an exciting prospect for teachers: 'It foregrounds professional experimentation and innovation and the quality outcomes achieved serve as an incentive' (Eyre, 2009a, p. 1053).

Measuring progress towards success

In High Performance Learning current levels of individual performance are seen as a 'snapshot in time', not as an unalterable predicator of future outcomes. We do need to look at progress, but not just progress alone. We also need always to be looking backwards at the distance travelled, but also forward at the distance between where the student is now and high performance; at what the gap is and how they can improve their personal best and gradually erode that gap, not just at the next short-term step. Imagine you were looking to run a marathon. Even though you can run only 2 miles when you begin training, you need to know that a marathon requires 26 miles. This enables you to measure your progress in closing the gap as well as in terms of progress from your last run. Personal bests are a stepping stone on the road to a defined destination, not an end in themselves.

So in a High Performance Learning school, setting by ability should not occur early. Even when a school creates 'sets' of students operating at a broadly similar level it is crucial that Set 2 is headed for the same destination as Set 1 – although perhaps by following a different or slower route. This is completely different from traditional schooling where Set 2 represents an acceptance that these students are not good enough to reach the dizzy heights identified for Set 1 and accordingly a less ambitious target is set. In High Performance Learning we consider that all students can eventually reach the dizzy heights – even if it takes longer and more practice for some – but if you remove the opportunity to do so, they simply cannot. School is stopping them from achieving.

Where should advanced learning occur?

Advanced learning opportunities can occur anywhere and at any time; the more, the better. The key to achieving advanced cognitive performance is that children and young people need to learn *how* to learn effectively and be encouraged to *want* to learn so that they will make maximum use of as many opportunities as possible. Formal schooling both in mainstream classes and in extra-curricular or enrichment time offers the opportunity to teach and practise the skills, but informal learning, in which the student may be learning independently, outside formal school, alone, online or with friends or interest groups, often provides ample opportunity to perfect those skills. This is why people who have a love of a subject and pursue it for pleasure make so much progress. School needs to be seen to value a child's learning even when they have not had a hand in directly guiding it. This is not always the case in school. Sometimes a student bringing in additional knowledge can be seen by teachers as challenging their authority or distracting the group from the syllabus. Instead, they are adding to the overall knowledge and creating new interest.

Motivation: no-one gets Willy Wonka's Golden Ticket to success

Much has been written about motivation. In particular, the positive psychology movement has focused attention on the conditions we need for well-being and effective functioning as opposed to looking at remedies for dysfunction or lack of motivation. This focus on the positive is exactly what we need to embrace in the quest for high performance for the majority. We need actively to motivate people to strive to do well and then support them to do it. We need them to understand that no-one is born with the magic ticket that guarantees success.

The work of people like Csikszentmihalyi (1990), who looks at when we do our best work, and Ryan and Deci (2000), who outline factors that lead to self-regulation and intrinsic motivation, are key to our increasing motivation in greater numbers of students. At the classroom level this can be expressed in a more straightforward way. Marcelo Staricoff (Balfour Primary School, Brighton) introduces even his youngest children to the concept of 'JONK', the joy-of-not-knowing. This serves to position all learning as an adventure in which periods of confusion and struggle are a natural part rather than a failure of personal aptitude.

Richard Feynman, the Nobel Prize winning physicist (Gleick, 1992) whose school IQ test placed him (inaccurately) as a respectable but unexceptional 125, found his conventional schooling to be an 'intellectual desert' and trained himself in algebra at home. Where he did encounter the requisite intellectual challenge was in the algebra club, which competed in New York's High School Interscholastic Algebra League. Here the approach was enquiry-based and competitive, which played strongly to his curiosity and thirst for knowledge.

This example does not indicate that mainstream schooling is of limited value and that after-school interest-led clubs are the route to success, but rather that mainstream schooling could benefit from a different pedagogy with a more enquiry-based approach that fosters the development of thinking as opposed to routine skills and knowledge transmission. Viewing each new topic as a question or problem to be investigated is more appealing and creates intrinsic motivation for the many. We all like to play detective. This example also demonstrates the value of enrichment activities and clubs, where greater time can be devoted to developing not only more sustained and complex work but also a deep love for the subject and its various dimensions. These two aspects of 'core' and 'extra', or 'co-curricula' schooling, are not separate; they are merely differing locations in which to build the advanced cognitive skills. We could and should add to that online as a third useful location for creating advanced learning opportunities. All are useful and should be encouraged.

For some students motivation is not a problem – they are interested in doing something because it is interesting, challenging and absorbing. They are largely self-starters and will persist even when the conditions are hostile, but they are the minority. Feynman was prepared to tolerate school and was fortunate to find an outlet eventually for his interests. Most students are not so tolerant. They lose interest if they find school boring and cease to strive for success. We need to make school more active and engaging for students, but we also need to teach *all* of them to persevere when the opportunities are not ideal because the journey to high performance usually includes persisting when things go wrong as well as celebrating when they go right.

It is worth thinking about motivation and discussing it in school. Traditionally in education we have used the carrot and stick approach to encourage students and deter them from making bad choices. We have hoped that some students would be intrinsically motivated, like Feynman, and have offered rewards and bribes for those who are not. However, it may be that motivation is more complex and that we could do more to help more students become intrinsically motivated. This would enable more students to achieve highly. Daniel Pink (2009) suggests that: 'The most successful people are not pursuing success for its own sake but rather working hard to control their lives, learn about their world and accomplish something that endures' (p. 79). See Figure 2.2.

He concludes that we can teach or at least encourage and enhance motivation if we focus on the three elements that motivate most people: Autonomy, Mastery and Purpose.

Everyone needs support

It is when learning proves a struggle that support becomes very important. When you do not believe in yourself and doubt your own capabilities you need someone else to encourage you. Everyone, no matter how exalted, reaches moments in their learning journey when they struggle. Whether they give up or push on through is one of the most critical decision points.

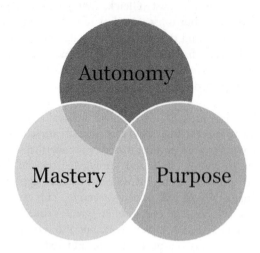

Figure 2.2 Motivation

Source: adapted from Pink (2009).

Sometimes it is when something is new and difficult to grasp that it is tempting to give up and believe you can never master it. But equally, it can be much later in the progress journey when things have been going well that they suddenly get harder and more difficult to conquer. Talking to successful adults, it emerges clearly that they can all recall these moments and the crucial decision taken then not to give up (see Figure 2.3).

Support for children sometimes comes from the family, while at other times it is a teacher or teachers at school, or then again it might be someone in the extended network who acts as a mentor. Family is often important; we all know about the influence of Mozart's father or Andy Murray's mother, but even in the household of Richard Feynman it was his father who ignited and nurtured his natural curiosity. But as students get older their support network is increasingly likely to include friends as well as family. These individuals are hugely important in the support network, especially in adolescence. Every successful person can point to the people who offered support at crucial moments and who created the confidence to succeed.

> Teachers are often the people who inspire us the most. I know I wouldn't be where I am today without my fourth grade teacher, Mrs. Duncan. She so believed in me, and for the first time, made me embrace the idea of learning. I learned to love learning because of Mrs. Duncan.
>
> (Oprah Winfrey, journalist and celebrity)

So when we look at why some people do not achieve highly, a relevant factor is the lack of a significant person/s with appropriate expectations of what could be achieved and who stands alongside the student as coach or mentor. In just the same way as in training musicians or sports people a significant mentor is a necessary prerequisite. Very few of us can make it entirely on our own.

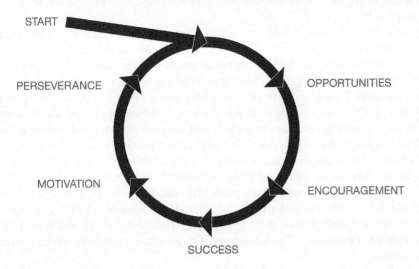

Figure 2.3 The learning journey

This factor is definitely one worth considering in relation to socio-economic and cultural barriers. Annette Lareau (2011), in her qualitative longitudinal work on race, class and family life, points to a middle-class parenting style which she calls 'concerted cultivation'. These parents leave nothing to chance. They encourage their children to talk back to them and negotiate, so building a personal confidence and style. They fight for their child if they do not make the top set and challenge the school. They schedule worthy activities and opportunities for their children to acquire new skills. By contrast, poor parents were found to adopt a less interventionist approach, seeing their responsibility as needing to care for their children but letting them grow and develop on their own.

So it is important to spell out to families the role they can and should play in terms of expectations of their children. Too little support or lack of belief in the child signals failure in terms of self-belief and will lead to underachievement, but equally a lifetime researching into gifted education convinces me that too much 'concerted intervention' can be a negative concept. 'Tiger Mums' or parents who put their children under pressure rarely see it producing the desired outcome in the long term because it is not the student making the journey, it is the parent pushing them and sooner or later they will rebel.

More positively, we know that encouraging parents to play an active role in their child's schooling can contribute to creating high performance (Jeynes, 2005): 'An analysis of over 300,000 K-12 students found that increased parental involvement is associated with substantially higher student achievement.'

Yet we should equally not disadvantage children whose parents are not in a position to offer this support. We must not make the harnessing of the power of parents yet another mechanism for disadvantaging the already disadvantaged.

Significant adults do not need to be from the family – that is merely the most convenient source of support. They can come from anywhere, and advice and support can emerge from more than one source or change at different stages in a child's life. What is important is that every student should feel they have someone who plays this role at various times in their life.

It is interesting to note that 'virtual' coaches have been found to work well with adults. Even the act of filling in weight loss information on an online chart and receiving feedback has been found to motivate and lead to better results when it comes to reducing obesity. In this respect, the emerging methodologies applied in the adult world have much to offer us in education. Finally, peer-to-peer coaching and support can be a useful part of the mix. Hattie (2008) suggests that feedback is a very significant factor in achievement. Feedback by peers can be given more frequently and sometimes with good understanding of the task and its possibilities. This does of course require training for it to be effective – especially when children are using this technique – but adult learners use feedback from peers as a primary form of feedback and it has considerable benefit, not least because they are fellow strugglers in the quest to master particular concepts.

The critical factor is that in order for us to create large numbers of high performing students we need to ensure that all these conditions for success are well and truly established rather than left to chance. The school needs to plan its approach to ensure delivery of all three aspects.

This may all seem like a large ask, but imagine what it would be like to have half or three-quarters of the school reaching heights that were previously only scaled by a small minority.

Notes

1 Stanford-Binet intelligence test.
2 Available online at http://www.brainyquote.com.

References

BBC Radio. (2015). *Desert Island Discs*. Kirsty Young, BBC Radio 4. First broadcast Friday 6 February, 09:00.
Bloom, B. S. (1982). The role of gifts and markers in the development of talent. *Exceptional Children*, 48(6), 510–522.
Csikszentmihalyi, M. (1990). *Flow: The Psychology of Optimal Experience*. New York: HarperCollins, Australia.
Eyre, D. (1997). *Able Children in Ordinary Schools*. London: David Fulton Publishers.
Eyre, D. (2007). *Gifted and Talented: What Really Works*. Warwick: National Academy for Gifted and Talented Youth. Available at: http://www.brightonline.org.uk/what_really_works.pdf.
Eyre, D. (2009a). The English model of gifted education. In L. V. Shavinina (ed.), *The International Handbook on Giftedness*. New York: Springer, pp. 1045–1059. doi:org/10.1007/978-1-4020-6162-2_53.
Eyre, D. (ed.) (2009b). *Major Themes in Gifted and Talented Education* (4 volumes). London: Routledge.
Eyre, D. and McClure, L. (2001). *Curriculum Provision for the Gifted and Talented in the Primary School: English, Math, Science, ICT* (NACE/Fulton Publication). London: David Fulton Publishers in association with the National Association for Able Children in Education.
Gleick, J. (1992). *Genius: R. Feynman*. London: Little, Brown and Company (UK).
Greenfield, S. (2014). *Mind Change*. London: Random House.
Guilford, J. P. (1967). *The Nature of Human Intelligence*. New York: McGraw-Hill.
Hattie, J. (2008). *Visible Learning*. London: Routledge.
Henshon, S. E. (2008). Adventurous navigator of the dimensions of high ability: An interview with Robert J. Sternberg. *Roeper Review*, 30(2), 75–80.

Jaeggi, S. M., Buschkuehl, M., Jonides, J. and Perrig, W. J. (2008). Improving fluid intelligence with training on working memory. *Proceedings of the National Academy of Sciences of the United States of America*, 105(19), 6829–6833. doi:10.1073/pnas.0801268105.

Jeynes, W. H. (2005). A meta-analysis of the relation of parental involvement to urban elementary school student academic achievement. *Urban Education*, 40 (May), 237–269.

Lareau, A. (2003). *Unequal Childhoods: Class, Race, and Family Life*. Berkeley: University of California Press.

Lohman, D. F. and Korb, K. A. (2006). Gifted today but not tomorrow? Longitudinal changes in ability and achievement during elementary school. *Journal for the Education of the Gifted*, 29(4), 451–486.

Open University (2015). *Our Story*. Available at: http://www.open.ac.uk/about/main/strategy/ou-story.

Pink, D. H. (2009). *Drive*. New York: Riverhead Books.

Ryan, R. M. and Deci, E. L. (2000). Intrinsic and extrinsic motivations: Classic definitions and new directions. *Contemporary Educational Psychology*, 25, 54–67.

Shore, B. M. (2000). Metacognition and flexibility: Qualitative differences in how gifted children think. In R. C. Friedman and B. M. Shore (eds), *Talents Unfolding: Cognition and Development*. Washington, DC: American Psychological Association.

Sternberg, R. J. (2010). WICS: A new model for cognitive education. *Journal of Cognitive Education & Psychology*, 9(1), 36–47.

Terman, L. (1925). *Genetic Studies of Genius*, Volume 1, *Mental and Physical Traits of a Thousand Gifted Children*. Stanford, CA: Stanford University Press.

Whyte, G. (2015). *Achieve the Impossible*. London: Bantam Press.

Chapter 3

The High Performance Learning framework

High Performance Learning *theory* assumes that most students are indeed capable of achieving the high levels of academic performance once seen as the domain of the very few and that the role of a school is to help the vast majority of their students to achieve at that level. It is about high performance for the many, not the few. The High Performance Learning *framework* is the way in which this theory can be converted into practical action at the school level and create world-leading schools. It teaches students how to develop greater intelligence.

At the heart of the framework are the ACPs (Advanced Cognitive Performance characteristics) and the VAAs (Values, Attitudes and Attributes). The ACPs are the ways of *thinking* that students need to develop. This is how we build better brains. This process can start very early and continue throughout primary and secondary school and beyond. There are twenty ACPs, which have been derived from the psychology, giftedness and neuroscience fields of study and these are grouped into five groups. They are the building blocks for high performance. Students need to aim, over time, to become fluent in them all.

Students can progress in these skills (see Appendix 2) and that progression can be assessed, but it is not age related. Some people will quickly make good progress in all or some of the skills, but others will take longer to acquire them. This is not a race. Some will need to practise these skills frequently in order to be confident enough to use them independently and that is fine, as long as they keep practising over time until they are secure. What is important is that students generally are aware of their usefulness and that individual students are aware of their own strengths and of areas that need more work.

Teachers should introduce students and their parents to the ACPs and then try to incorporate these into lesson tasks and help students to recognise when a task would benefit from the use of a skill. It is not the intention that one lesson should focus on one skill and next lesson on another, but rather that this overall suite of skills is evident in lessons where appropriate, is mentioned and used regularly and frequently.

For the teacher, the ACPs provide a systematic framework for the development of advanced learning – higher order thinking opportunities. Many schools already use higher order thinking, especially with the most able students, but unlike earlier models such as Bloom's Taxonomy (Bloom, 1985), these characteristics are an up-to-date, comprehensive set and have progression routes built into them. Similarly to other sets of higher order thinking skills, these skills are generic but some lend themselves more readily to particular subjects.

For the student they are the road map that enables them to play a more active role in their own learning and become more autonomous. By introducing the ACPs to learners and making them visible in the school you enable them to try out skills and practise them on their own. A 'eureka' moment for me was hearing some top primary students using the term 'flexible thinking' (an ACP) in the playground game they had set up. This demonstrated their familiarity with the concept and its uses plus their ability and fluency in applying it even in their social life.

Coupled with the ACPs are the VAAs. These are the ways of *behaving* that the learner needs to acquire. There are ten VAAs grouped into three groups, again with possible progression (see Appendix 4). It is the use of two together that makes for success. They are the 'double helix'. Neither will deliver success alone, but together they create high performers. They focus on the facets of character and personality that characterise effective, holistic learners. These include the key characteristics of perseverance and resilience, but also enterprise, global awareness and concern for others.

These should work alongside the ACPs and underpin the way in which the curriculum is approached and taught. Drawing the attention of students to the ACPs helps them to realise that high performance is not a result of being destined by birth for success, but rather the result of learning appropriate skills plus effort and hard work. They will also understand that if you succeed, this success comes with the responsibility to make the world around you a better place.

The VAAs are more familiar to teachers than the ACPs because a variety of lists of these kinds of behaviours already exist. What is unique to high performance is that (a) the progression routes within the VAAs have been identified, so students can progress and be assessed if required, and (b) that they are being used in conjunction with the ACPs rather than as a separate educational approach. This integrated approach reflects the way in which good school systems work. They focus on the simple and manageable and make this work well, rather than asking teachers to juggle multiple agendas and programmes.

By introducing the ACPs and VAAs to parents you make explicit what the school is trying to achieve and you create a shared language between school and family. Schools which reward progress in these skills by sending home certificates or a video or photos help parents in this way to see what is important in building learning capability. Parents become better equipped to play their role when they too can help in the quest to build these characteristics through the way they raise their children.

The supporting pillars

While the ACPs and VAAs form the language and basis of High Performance Learning, there is a range of factors that help to ensure that when building the ACPs and VAAs you create the best possible climate for success. These are called the supporting pillars and there are seven of them (see Figure 3.1).

I Mindset shift

The correct mindset is a precondition for High Performance Learning. Unless you believe that ability is flexible and can be developed, none of this will occur. It is easy to introduce this idea into school as part of in-service training and to gain superficial acceptance. This makes sense and is in many ways attractive. But when people begin to see that it will mean a radical adjustment to their current professional behaviours they are often more reluctant and more sceptical about embracing the approach. They will point to

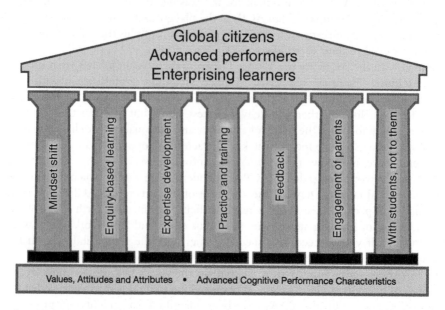

Figure 3.1 The seven pillars of high performance

individuals who are currently achieving poorly and doubt their ability to do better. This is not helpful. Believing in people's ability to develop into high performers does not mean that you can wave a magic wand and everyone will be transformed. By embarking on High Performance Learning a school is committing to a journey that expects more of itself and students, and year on year delivers that with increasing levels of efficiency. As we established in a project in Saudi Arabia (Mawhiba Schools Partnership, King Abdulaziz and his Companions Foundation for Giftedness and Creativity), making this change is a marathon rather than a sprint and will take 3 to 5 years to achieve maximum impact in any school. However, progress culturally and with individuals is visible almost at once and exam results start to improve quickly.

2 Enquiry-based learning

When it comes to academic performance, it is not just a question of 'what' is taught but also 'how' it is taught. Not just 'knowledge' but also 'pedagogy'. The basic curriculum needs to be a demanding one that places a significant cognitive demand on students. The pedagogy needs to be enquiry based so as to encourage independent thought and build intellectual confidence.

The question in High Performance Learning is how to teach in a way that best embeds the higher level learning skills. Enquiry-based learning is an approach by which new learning usually starts with a question or questions that lead to an investigation. The teacher is attempting to make the student curious and motivated to find the answer or master the concept. Students are often already actively engaged in problem-solving and research and this provides excellent opportunities to develop the ACPs and VAAs and will inevitably form a significant part of the overall mix.

High Performance Learning assumes a broadly constructionist approach[1] to education in which students are building their own academic capability, guided by teachers. This does not dictate or preclude any specific teaching methodology, i.e. lectures can be perfect for learning new information fast while exploratory learning can lead to a deeper understanding, so the use of both is valuable. What is important is that learning is student focused and success from the teaching perspective is measured by the learning acquired by individual students rather than what the teacher does.

During schooling, students need to acquire a combination of strong subject knowledge and the ability to use and apply it wisely. Placing one concept at the centre and aligning the other accordingly is not easy for the teacher. In short, subject-based curricula require the addition of a skills-based pedagogy, while skills-based curricula need systematically to insert content in a sequential and increasingly sophisticated way. This complexity is the reason why many countries have moved to a national curriculum or at least a common core, which secures that basic entitlement of knowledge and concepts for all students.

Enquiry-based learning does not suggest a lack of attention to knowledge; rather, it addresses how the knowledge is secured. In recent years there have been various debates about the value of teaching knowledge. It is beguiling to think that because knowledge is now so easily and readily available it is no longer important to teach it. Just a little thought renders that argument invalid. If you have very limited knowledge and have to rely on looking up information, first it is slow and time consuming, and second you are not well placed to make connections between existing pieces of knowledge and that is how you solve problems and acquire new and original ideas (Jerome Bruner in Boswell, 1967). Indeed, research into more advanced cognitive performance suggests that the more knowledge and skills you can recall or use without thought – automaticity – the more you will progress. So to reduce knowledge is to disadvantage students, and the way technology creates ready access to additional knowledge should be seen as a bonus, rather than a replacement of traditional methods.

Much work has been done on the use of enquiry to develop higher order thinking (Renzulli, 1988; Fisher, 1992; Maker and Nielson, 1995; Eyre, 1997; Van Tassel-Baska and Brown, 2007; MaCabe Mowat, 2008; Smith, Lovatt and Turner, 2009) and many practical examples and teaching models already exist to assist teachers and learners. Almost all of these can usefully assist in generating ideas for tasks that will build specific ACPs and VAAs. In addition, the associations supporting gifted education in various countries such as the National Association for Able Children in Education (NACE) in the UK and the National Association for Gifted Children in the USA have excellent practical resources available for teachers.

3 Expertise development

Advanced cognitive performance is defined not just as passing exams, although this is a positive feature that always occurs, but instead as the components associated with expertise as set out within a given domain, for example maths. This focus on the development of expertise enables students to perform well not only in school but beyond it at university and later in life because they have achieved a level of learning mastery which enables them to operate independently and effectively.

Expertise development may be defined in layman's terms as not just covering the curriculum but developing the habits and behaviours associated with expertise in a given domain. For example, thinking and approaching tasks like a mathematician or a historian rather than just doing the maths or a history course. This of course has significant implications for how lessons are taught. It means that you might encourage very young students to weigh evidence in the same way as you do in history at GCSE or consider literary theory in upper secondary as opposed to university. These are skills that signify growing expertise in the subject and students find it very enjoyable to be apprentices on the road to becoming experts rather than merely 'covering the curriculum'.

This concept of subject mastery is not new. Bloom developed an approach to this in 1968 with his Learning for Mastery and in 1971 with Mastery Learning (Bloom, 1974). He suggested that people learn at different rates and that the curriculum should be broken down into small units and taught in different ways to enable different kinds of students to succeed. The core of his approach was *Feedback, Correctives and Enrichment.* Teachers were to provide individual students with frequent and specific feedback on their learning progress through regular, formative classroom assessments. This feedback was intended to be both diagnostic and prescriptive. Where necessary it would include corrective activity, and if students were already demonstrating mastery, enrichment would be provided. In reality this was an early form of differentiation with assessment for learning at its heart. What was interesting here was the idea that students focused on mastery of the subject or topic and their journey towards it, not just on subject coverage.

Much later, Ericsson and colleagues (Van Gog *et al.*, 2005) embarked on an extensive set of work around the more holistic concept of 'expertise development'. This was focused not on mastering small components but on the bigger concept of overall mastery of a domain or subject – becoming expert. In a range of studies he has looked at the journey to expert performance. His empirical studies have given us a good understanding of how individuals develop expertise in specific domains and why this approach is superior to more conventional, comprehension-based school learning. High Performance Learning owes much to his work. The ACPs and VAAs use this approach and identify the characteristics associated with cognitive expertise in school. They outline the journey to expertise in a generic sense but this can be supplemented by subject-specific skills. On the cognitive journey it is difficult to determine what full-blown expertise would look like, but mastery of the ACPs and VAAs would make an excellent start.

This focus on expertise, or mastery, of the subject domain is helpful in characterising the nature of good education provision. It helps to establish what we are aiming for. In essence, all students are on the journey from novice to expert. Some students will of course progress more quickly and some may never reach the higher levels, but if we can identify the characteristics of expertise in a particular subject domain it is possible to start to consider how best to nurture it. We can also explore whether there are clearly identifiable milestones on the journey.

4 Practice and training

So once you have the route map to expertise (and hence high academic performance), the question is how to ensure that greater numbers of people complete the whole journey. Through his work over 20 years, Ericsson has sought empirical evidence that shows that superior performance is indeed reproducible and he is increasingly confident that it is. His work in psychology is now arriving at the same conclusion as the neuroscientists (Jonides *et al.*, 2012), that superior performance can be taught. Ericsson, along with others, is clear that extended deliberate practice (e.g. high concentration practice beyond one's comfort zone) has been found to play a significant role. Experts become expert because they are prepared to put in the necessary work and to persevere when they meet obstacles in their subject. They are motivated to do that because they have developed a sense of the subject and that in turn leads to a love of the subject. So exploring the nature and conventions of a subject is key to developing expertise within it.

> The research on expert performance has, I believe, demonstrated convincingly that neither a magical bullet nor an innate talent can allow someone to attain an expert level of performance rapidly and effortlessly. Even for the most 'talented' individuals, the road to excellence takes many years of daily deliberate practice to acquire the complex mechanisms and adaptations that mediate expert performance and its continued maintenance and improvement.
>
> (Ericsson *et al.*, 2007)

This idea of practice being the key to success has captured something of the public imagination – not least because popularist authors such as Malcolm Gladwell (2009) have identified famous case studies where this is certainly evident – The Beatles, Bill Gates, and others. Practice is a useful concept in school because it helps students to persevere. If the rhetoric of the school is constantly stressing that rewards come as the result of effort and practice – rather than natural ability or aptitude – then putting in the effort becomes more convincing for the student.

However, practice is not the same as experience and just doing something repeatedly will not automatically lead to improvement: 'Deliberate practice must be distinguished from mere experience, in that only through focusing and improving specific aspects of performance, such as the aspects in which the performer is weakest, can an aspiring individual improve' (Ericsson *et al.*, 2007).

So it is focused practice that is required as opposed to random practice. Badly planned remedial work has been found sometimes to reinforce errors (Ward, 2003), and so it is not just practice, but the right practice that is needed and should be focused on the ACPs.

5 Feedback

Of course effective practice is related to good feedback. You need to know what to practise in order to improve. Like practice, feedback needs to be targeted and constructive if it is to be useful in raising academic performance.

The importance of effective feedback is not a new idea, but it has come into sharper focus in recent years with the growing interest in personalisation and the findings from John Hattie's work which identifies feedback as the single most effective classroom intervention (Hattie, 2008).

Hattie focuses on the process of feedback and points out (Hattie and Timperley, 2007, p. 87) that there are different types of feedback with some being more effective than others (Harks *et al.*, 2014). Effectiveness can be enhanced by following his process outlined in Figure 3.2.

Hattie's (southern hemisphere based) interest in feedback has coincided with the Assessment for Learning movement drawing on the work of Black and Williams (1998; London based), which has become widely adopted in the UK. Assessment for Learning focuses on the ways in which formative assessment can be deployed in the classroom

Feedback to enhance learning

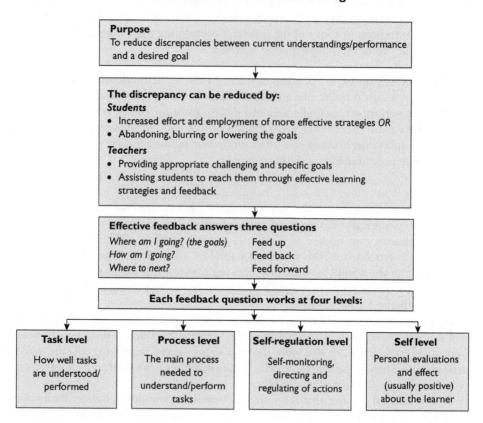

Figure 3.2 Feedback

Source: Hattie and Timperley, 2007, p. 87.

through the use of practical strategies and techniques. Teachers can use these to improve the quality of evidence based on which they, and their students, make instructional decisions and so enable better progress. Assessment for Learning was described by the Assessment Reform Group (2002) as the process of seeking and interpreting evidence for use by learners and their teachers to decide where the learners are in their learning, where they need to go and how best to get there (www.aaia.org.uk). Broadfoot and coworkers (1999) characterised this as:

- being an essential part of teaching and learning;
- sharing learning goals with pupils;
- helping pupils to know and recognise the standards they are aiming for;
- involving pupils in self-assessment;
- providing feedback which leads to pupils recognising their next steps and how to take them;
- being underpinned by confidence that every student can improve;
- involving both teacher and pupils in reviewing and reflecting on assessment data.

Practical examples of how to use feedback and assessment for learning in the classroom are now readily available online and in print. In High Performance Learning feedback and assessment for learning are important concepts in the overall approach, but for them to meet the High Performance Learning criteria they must be combined with high expectations of what the student can achieve. They should not merely be a focus on good progress given the child's innate ability, but rather focus on setting demanding ambitions for future accomplishments.

All of the above is focused on enhancing cognition (ACPs), but in High Performance Learning we are also concerned with character and personality (VAAs). So feedback needs not only to enhance cognitive ability but also confidence and well-being. This aspect of feedback is often overlooked (Voerman et al., 2014), but can be critical in terms of building motivation and persistence. It means that feedback will usually include both comments on progress and comments on the gap between current performance and optimal performance and will always be phrased in terms of what needs to happen next as opposed to remonstrating against what has not happened. In addition, it must instil in the child a growing sense of confidence about what it is realistically possible for him or her to achieve.

Woodard (2011, p. 383) sums this up nicely when he describes Ericsson's theory as based on:

> Seeking continual incremental growth (not aiming too high too soon), using targeted strategies directed at specific improvements, focused attention to avoid going on 'cruise control' (using the same methods continually without critical evaluation), use of a coach or mentor to create tasks and provide feedback on successes and failures.

Feedback can come from teacher (coach) to student or from peer to peer. This helps to set the next destination and to encourage self-regulation. Before they receive feedback from others it is useful to ask students to assess themselves on the task.

Overall, it is worth the school's spending significant time on the question of feedback within the parameters of the High Performance Learning approach. It can be a real driver for fast progress at the whole-school level.

6 Engagement with parents

In the international studies on effective schools, Epstein and associates (2002) identify strong parental engagement as being a feature of the best schools. This is hardly surprising; indeed, the best schools involve all the community in helping to educate the child and parents are a primary source of support.

Most parents are keen to help their child to do well, even when they have not been successful at school themselves or when they do not feel confident as to how to do this. Equally, very successful adults are often novice parents and some find parenting very difficult. Yet, if the child is to succeed, having the parents and school working in harmony can significantly improve the chance of success. From the school's point of view it is worth noting that many parents, even those who are well educated, can find school intimidating. Perhaps it is because they have all been to school themselves as students and find it difficult to move into the more equal role of parent. Certainly, the first time I visited the head teacher's office as a teacher it felt very daunting, because previous head teacher visits had been largely as a student to receive a reprimand. So for schools to become world class they need to be generally and proactively welcoming to parents and keep them informed and involved so that they feel they are truly a part of the school.

High Performance Learning stresses the benefits of parental involvement at all ages, not just in the school but more importantly in their child's own learning, whether it be with young children, who are usually curious but may not yet be well disciplined, or older students, who may worry about their work, their capabilities and their future. The High Performance Learning framework of ACPs and VAAs makes it very simple to involve parents in their child's learning in a way that is clear and straightforward. It provides a language, tells the parents that this is what the school is about, and provides the reassurance of knowing that regardless of current performance their child is on track to do well.

In discussions with parents in High Performance Learning schools, they seem to be particularly committed and interested in their child's learning. But they are also unafraid to talk openly with teachers about the barriers that are preventing their child from doing well. This is because they know that the shared agenda is about removing the barriers that inhibit success rather than about apportioning blame.

Both primary (elementary) and secondary (high) schools can play a proactive role in suggesting to parents ways in which they might work with and support their child. These ideas may seem obvious to us as teachers but they are not always obvious to parents.

7 With learners, not to them

The whole of the High Performance Learning framework is about helping students to develop their capabilities – helping them to become effective learners who will achieve highly. So it is essential that the school positions High Performance Learning as an activity in which students are encouraged to take responsibility for their own learning, are actively involved and make decisions.

As for parents, having the overall framework and the ACPs and VAAs as the building blocks enables students to know what they need to be able to do if they are to enhance their chances of success. It makes the process transparent. Of course, with young children it is helpful to focus on a subset of characteristics instead of all of them in order to make this manageable. This is one of the aspects that a school needs to address when implementing High Performance Learning strategies.

In adopting High Performance Learning, it is useful for the school to agree how it will signal its expectation of increased and proactive participation by the student. This should be done both by talking directly to students and also through adjustments to the systems and processes. For example, by considering where such additional participation will take place and when. Many schools say that they already involve students in their own learning, but this approach requires something of a sea change in which students are sufficiently involved so as to feel they are in control of their own learning journey and are clear about what they need to do next.

Where does all this lead?

High Performance Learning sets out to create students whose profile includes traditional academic success, but it also creates a certain type of student who will be college-ready, workplace-ready and life-ready.

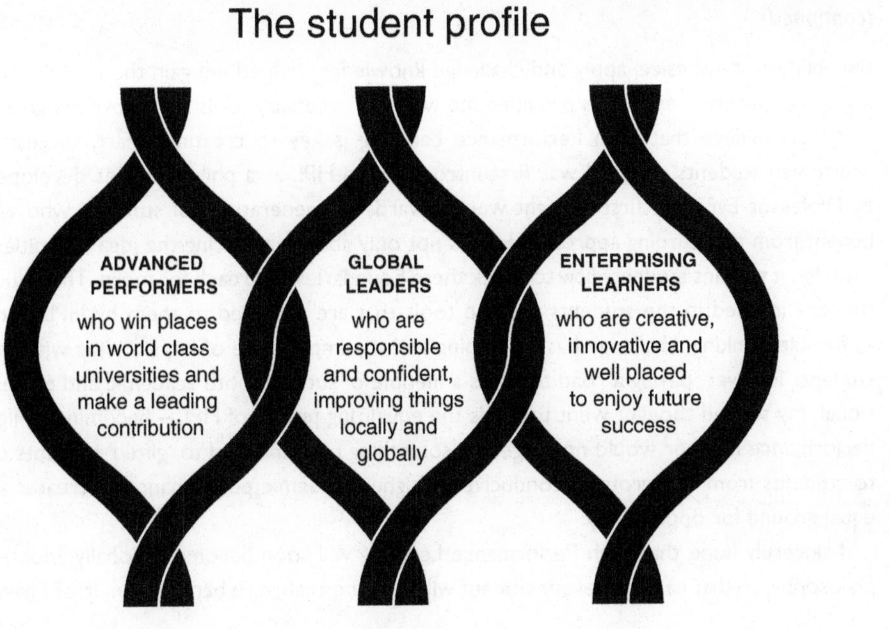

The student profile

Figure 3.3 Profile of a high performing student

These students will be academic high performers who can choose their post-school destination from a strong position of academic success. They will also be responsible and confident and keen to improve the world around them locally and globally. They will be individuals who are creative and innovative, not afraid to try new ideas or bring forward new thoughts. In short, they will be well prepared to deal with the unexpected and whatever the future holds (see Figure 3.3).

Case study

My name is Linda Phan, and I graduated from The British School, Warsaw in May 2015 and am going on to Columbia University. Personally, I have always embraced the foundational values of High Performance Learning (HPL) – the idea that there is no limit to a student's potential, and that academic performance can best be improved through practice and perseverance. Throughout primary school, I had often underachieved; nevertheless, instead of letting their doubts take over, my teachers and parents continued to encourage me and help me develop a positive mindset towards learning and achievement. This played a paramount role in my growth as a learner; entering secondary school, I was the top student in my class. In secondary school, HPL jumpstarted my development as a leader, both in the classroom and outside of it; acquiring valuable skills (e.g. independent thinking and

(continued)

(continued)

the ability to synthesize, apply and challenge knowledge) helped me gain the confidence I needed to succeed, as well as provided me with the necessary tools to achieve my goals.

I truly believe that High Performance Learning is key to creating smart, successful and driven students. When I was first introduced to HPL as a philosophy, as developed by Professor Eyre, my first thought went towards the generations of students who will benefit from the learning approach. HPL is not only about embracing the idea of limitless capacity, it teaches students *how* to break these boundaries and reach for more. The values that are instilled in the students and the tools that are provided to them by HPL, such as flexible thinking, challenge-based learning and the importance of inquiry, stay with the students for ever, paving a road towards a lifetime of success, both academic and professional. My second thought went towards the equalizing power of HPL – becoming a High Performance Learner would no longer be something only afforded to 'gifted' students or to students from backgrounds conducive to higher academic performance. It creates an equal ground for opportunity.

I sincerely hope that High Performance Learning will soon become a globally adopted philosophy, so that each and every student will have the chance to benefit from it, as I have.

Note

1 Learners constructing their own understanding and knowledge of the world, through experiencing things and reflecting on those experiences.

References

Black, P. and Williams, D. (1998). *Inside the Black Box: Raising Standards through Classroom Assessment.* London: Kings College.

Bloom, B. S. (1974). An introduction to mastery learning theory. In J. H. Block (ed.), *Schools, Society, and Mastery Learning.* New York: Holt, Rinehart & Winston.

Bloom, B. (ed.) and Sosniak, L. A. (1985). *Developing Talent in Young People.* New York: Random House Publishing Group.

Boswell, J. G. (1967). Out of the Garden of Eden, with Jerome Bruner. *Journal of Teacher Education,* 18(4), 463–469.

Broadfoot, P. M., Daugherty, R., Gardner, J., Gipps, C. V., Harlen, W., James, M. and Stobart, G. (1999). *Assessment for Learning: Beyond the Black Box.* Cambridge, UK: University of Cambridge School of Education.

Epstein, J., Sanders, M., Sheldon, S., Simon, B. S., Salinas, K. C., Jansorn, N. R., Van Voorhis, F. L., Martin, C. S., Thomas, B. G., Greenfield, M. D., Hutchins, D. J. and Williams, K. J. (2002). *School, Family and Community Partnerships, Your Handbook for Action,* 2nd edn. California: Corwin Press.

Ericsson, K. A., Roring, R. W. and Nandagopal, K. (2007). Misunderstandings, agreements, and disagreements: Toward a cumulative science of reproducibly superior aspects of giftedness. *High Ability Studies,* 18(1), 97–115. doi:10.1080/1359813070135108.

Eyre, D. (1997). *Able Children in Ordinary Schools.* London: David Fulton Publishers.

Fisher, R. (1992). *Teaching Children to Think.* Cheltenham: Stanley Thornes (Publishers) Ltd.

Gladwell, M. (2009). *Outliers: The Story of Success.* London: Penguin Group UK.

Harks, B., Rakoczy, K., Hattie, J., Besser, M. and Klieme, E. (2014). The effects of feedback on achievement, interest and self-evaluation: The role of feedback's perceived usefulness. *Educational Psychology*, 34(3), 269–290. doi:10.1080/01443410.2013.785384.

Hattie, J. (2008). *Visible Learning*. London: Routledge.

Hattie, J. and Timperley, H. (2007). The power of feedback. *Review of Educational Research*, 77(1), 1–112.

Jonides, J., Jaeggi, S. M., Buschkuehl, M. and Shah, P. (2012). Building better brains. *Scientific American Mind*, 23(4), 59–63.

MaCabe Mowat, A. (2008). *Brilliant Activities for Stretching Gifted and Talented Children*. Poole: Brilliant Publications.

Maker, C. and Nielson, A. (1995). *Teaching Models in Education of the Gifted*, 2nd edn. Texas: Pro–Ed.

Renzulli, J. S. (1988). The multiple menu model for developing differentiated curriculum for the gifted and talented. *Gifted Child Quarterly*, 32(3), 298–309.

Smith, A., Lovatt, M. and Turner, J. (2009). *Learning to Learn in Practice*. Carmarthen: Crown House Publishing.

Van Gog, T., Ericsson, K., Rikers, R. and Paas, F. (2005). Instructional design for advanced learners: Establishing connections between the theoretical frameworks of cognitive load and deliberate practice. *Educational Technology Research and Development*, 53(3), 73–81. Education Research Complete, EBSCO *host*, accessed 27 April 2015.

Van Tassel-Baska, J. and Brown, E. F. (2007). Toward best practice: An analysis of the efficacy of curriculum models in gifted education. *Gifted Child Quarterly*, 51(4), 342–358.

Voerman, L., Korthagen, F. J., Meijer, P. C. and Simons, R. J. (2014). Feedback revisited: Adding perspectives based on positive psychology. Implications for theory and classroom practice. *Teaching and Teacher Education*, 43, 91–98. doi:10.1016/j.tate.2014.06.005.

Ward, H. (2003). Booster classes for less able misfire. *TES: Times Educational Supplement*, 4561, 1.

Woodard, R. (2011). K. Anders Ericsson's theory of deliberate practice for expert performance in the senior Capstone course. *Teaching Theology and Religion*, 14(4), 382–383. doi:10.1111/j.1467-9647.2011.00741.x.

Chapter 4

The Advanced Cognitive Performance characteristics (ACPs)

The High Performance Learning approach identifies two core sets of characteristics that students must develop if they are to become academic high performers. These are the building blocks for developing advanced thinking and advanced learner behaviours. They are the DNA of the High Performance Learning framework and must become the DNA of the school. They are used in combination and need to become so much a part of the way the school operates that they become the language of the school used by students as well as staff and parents. Everyone must understand their significance and work towards becoming fluent users of the ACPs and VAAs. (See appendix 2 to 5). Acquiring these skills enables students to act more intelligently and perform more highly. When students use them effectively they must be rewarded and their use must become more sophisticated over time.

The first of these is the Advanced Cognitive Performance characteristics (ACPs). These are a set of twenty ways of *thinking* that are associated with advanced cognitive performance. The second set is the ten Values, Attitudes and Attributes (VAAs). These are the ways of learner *behaviours* that students need to exhibit. Using the ACPs and the VAAs in combination forms a double helix of competencies that enables most students to perform in the same advanced cognitive way as those labelled 'able' or 'gifted' students.

In the past, education has relied on the development of one or other of these sets of characteristics, whereas it is in fact their interplay that leads to the required outcome of advanced cognitive performance. Learning to think in advanced ways is critical, but that in itself is insufficient. It does nothing to ensure that the learner is a well rounded concerned citizen or to help develop the critical skills of persistence and practice that are so key to success. Therefore, it is important to become proficient in both elements as the ACPs relate to how to think, whereas the VAAs relate to ways of applying that thinking in creative and sensitive ways (see Figure 4.1).

It is not the intention that a school should offer special lessons in order to develop the ACPs and VAAs, but it does need to find ways to introduce and embed them and this will require a change project with appropriate goals and milestones. It needs a systematic rather than an *ad hoc* approach. Schools that have been most effective in terms of results have been those that think carefully about both the introduction stage and the embedding stage and ultimately including an audit of just how embedded and universal these have become in the systems and processes of the school.

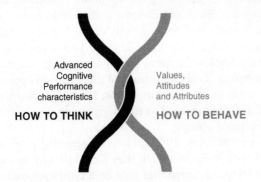

Advanced Cognitive Performance characteristics	Values, Attitudes and Attributes
HOW TO THINK	**HOW TO BEHAVE**

Figure 4.1 The two core strands

Introducing the advanced cognitive performance characteristics

In order to be successful academically it is necessary to acquire a repertoire of ways of thinking that enable you to make sense of information, to create new thoughts and to know how to approach and unscramble complex ideas.

Research into how gifted children think and learn indicates that these abilities are not unique to the gifted. They are a set of skills that can be learned by anyone. What makes the gifted appear gifted is that either they were introduced to them early and so appear advanced or that they demonstrate greater initial aptitude – although this is not always developed further over time: 'The state of the art seems to be that gifted children differ from others in the extent to which they draw on a repertoire of intellectual skills that are nonetheless available to others' (Shore, 2000).

Either way, it is possible to train more students to become familiar with this repertoire of advanced thinking skills and behaviours and to help them to become confident in their use. The vast majority of students spontaneously pick up some meta-cognitive knowledge and skills from their parents, their peers and particularly their teachers. But it is possible to teach these skills and enhance their use significantly (Veenman *et al.*, 1994).

Although there are some particular domain-specific cognitive skills, most research-ers suggest that the majority of these skills are generic. Some may lend themselves more readily to some subjects than others, but by teaching the generic set of ACPs students will be able to make effective use of those most appropriate to any given subject. Teachers of specific subjects generally find they use some more than others.

My own research into the key cognitive characteristics associated with gifted students (Eyre, 2009) confirmed that there was little dispute among academics about the range of characteristics associated with advanced cognitive performance. While individual items and precise groupings differ from researcher to researcher, a significant degree of consen-sus exists around the overall set of ideas. This is very helpful for teachers. The nature of the skills and behaviours is such that there is a degree of overlap, but it is possible to iden-tify a clear list of characteristics and that is what I have done in order to create the ACPs.

What is especially relevant here is that some students grow up under conditions that are favourable to the development of these critical and creative skills and so have a far greater chance of becoming proficient in them and consequently do well academically. These tend to be the children of well educated, middle-class families. This is one reason that these children are often thought in school to be more intelligent and are the most likely to be in top sets and 'gifted' programmes. Teaching advanced thinking – as opposed to leaving its acquisition to chance – is a practical intervention that, in conjunction with appropriate learner behaviours (VAAs), has the potential to transform attainment among traditionally socio-economically disadvantaged groups.

In the 1990s, some researchers (Shayer and Adey, 1993) did very interesting work on Cognitive Accelerated Science Education (CASE), in which they found that by making ways of thinking more explicit in their science programmes they could improve student performance not only in science but also more generally. They approached this topic by attributing certain kinds of thinking to certain kinds of tasks and teaching students which skill to use for which kind of task. This had some merit.

However, much of the work on pedagogy in gifted education suggests that what is needed is something a little more advanced. First, students do indeed need to gain a sense of the repertoire and when each approach is most likely to be used. But they then need to develop the intellectual confidence that allows them to select a non-conventional approach sometimes, or to change approach midstream if that seems useful. So instead of stopping at matching thinking skills to tasks, it would appear to be more useful to introduce individual skills and seek multiple opportunities to practise them, in the normal classroom and beyond, until that skill becomes a part of the lexicon. Deciding which thinking approach to use is part of the fun of learning and advanced learning is about fun. Using an unconventional approach is not wrong provided it works. Advanced cognitive performance is about flexibility of approach.

Shayer and Adey, along with most other proponents of the thinking skills movement of the 1990s, also failed to recognise the critical link with learner behaviours (our VAAs). A student can become adept at using advanced thinking, but that in itself is not enough. We know that, for example, the ability to persist when learning gets difficult is a key factor in eventual success, and so these learner behaviours or habits are equally important and must be used in conjunction with advanced thinking.

Gifted students who underachieve often are capable of using advanced thinking but do not apply it, either through lack of motivation or lack of confidence or lack of open-mindedness. Equally, much school learning focuses on delivering the 'right answer'. Underachievement among gifted students is frequently the result of being risk-averse and more concerned to retain the status of 'gifted' than to enjoy the learning journey with all its ups and downs. This is a direct consequence of focusing on fixed ability as opposed to current levels of performance.

The individual ACPs

The list of the twenty ACPs constitutes a breaking down of the various characteristics associated with advanced cognitive performance and subsequent representation in a form that can readily be used in ordinary classrooms without changing curriculum or organisational structures. Initially, these ACPs were compiled as a single list and I am indebted to

Stuart White and colleagues at the British International School Shanghai (Puxi) for usefully creating five grouping categories for their implementation with students, staff and parents: Meta-thinking, Linking, Analysing, Creating and Realising.

Meta-thinking

This first set of four characteristics relate to consciously thinking about thinking. They are the characteristics that help students to beware of the repertoire of thinking skills that is available to them and also the need for self-awareness in selecting which work best in which circumstances. This creates the intellectual confidence that enables students to tackle even difficult problems. Students will first be introduced to these skills, but right from the outset it helps to encourage them to think about circumstances in which each skill will be useful.

Meta-cognition

> *The ability to knowingly use a wide range of thinking approaches and to transfer knowledge from one circumstance to another.*

Meta-cognition was originally referred to (Brown, 1978; Flavell, 1979) as the knowledge about and regulation of one's cognitive activities in the learning process. Over time, this initial simple definition has been expanded and subdivided by psychologists, and as Veenman and coworkers (2006) point out, the term is now used to encompass meta-cognitive beliefs, meta-cognitive awareness, meta-cognitive experiences, meta-cognitive knowledge, feeling of knowing, judgement of learning, theory of mind, meta-memory, meta-cognitive skills, executive skills, higher order skills, meta-components, comprehension monitoring, learning strategies, heuristic strategies, and self-regulation.

In High Performance Learning (HPL) we return to the simple definition, which relates to conscious knowledge and transfer. First, this means being aware of the possible thinking approaches that might be useful in any given context and then knowingly using one of your choice. This could include taking an idea or skill learned in one subject and transferring it to a new context. This meta-cognition is at the heart of using and applying information and is a critical skill in advanced cognitive performance.

In the teaching environment it is possible to encourage the use of meta-cognition by drawing attention to this type of thinking and asking, for example, 'What kind of approach do you think we might use to solve this problem?'. This helps students become aware of and familiar with the concept.

Self-regulation

> *The ability to monitor, evaluate and self-correct.*

Self-regulation is essential in becoming an advanced cognitive performer (Zimmerman, 2008; Jarvela and Jarvenoja, 2011). It helps students to operate independently, to plan, monitor and assess their own learning. Ultimately, students are more likely to persist with a challenging task if they are in control of their learning. This is because they are more engaged in their learning and more motivated to succeed. Self-regulated learners are also more likely to seek out advice and support and will perform better on academic tests (Schunk and Zimmerman, 2007).

The term self-regulation includes goal setting and planning, but also learners using their own strategies, in addition to or instead of the recommended ones, to keep themselves on track. In order to self-regulate the student must learn how to self-monitor and be aware of his or her own progress towards his or her own goals. Students must also learn how to evaluate their learning and performance more broadly on any given task/s and make adjustments for future occasions. Schools can encourage self-regulation in three distinct ways. First, they can formally instruct or teach self-regulatory practices. Second, they can guide students to help them understand how to self-regulate and, third, they can create a school culture in which self-regulation is an expected and supported practice in all classes and at all ages. In all these instances we know from Assessment for Learning practices (Black and Williams, 1998) that progress will be best where feedback is frequent and targeted and operates in a social environment (Hattie and Timperley, 2007).

Some research has also been undertaken into the links between self-regulation and motivation (Wolters, 2011), not just to establish whether the two are linked but also to discover how students attempt to control their own motivation or motivational processing. This kind of knowledge can help with active management of their motivation or motivational processing.

Self-regulation cannot operate in isolation. It must form part of the overall set of meta-thinking activities, but it might be said that it is key to maximising the effectiveness of all the ACPs.

Strategy planning

The ability to approach new learning experiences by actively attempting to connect them to existing knowledge or concepts and hence determine an appropriate way to think about the work.

A major stumbling block for many students is that feeling of panic when you don't know how to begin. The task is large and confusing and many students just dive in at the start and try to work their way forward rather than looking at the whole requirement and then deciding how to approach it.

For example, my colleague Barry Teare used a task for in-service training based on the creation of a family tree. The worksheet listed all the relevant information needed to create the tree but not in the expected sequential order, so starting with the first piece of information was not valuable. In addition, he had added some extraneous information that was of no value at all. Using this task as a part of in-service training as well in the classroom with students it was interesting to see how different people approached it. Some did indeed make the classic mistake of trying to work sequentially through the data as set out. Others figured out quickly that this would not work and had to decide *how* to approach the task. In doing so, they drew on their existing knowledge of how they had approached similar data tasks and been successful.

Teaching students to recognise that the task is a complex one is important; and then to recognise that there is no need to panic – just to think out a way to approach it, perhaps by using a technique you have used before. A fun way to help students become more confident with this is sometimes to approach a complex task as a whole-class activity. Introduce the task, ask pairs of students to think, pair and share their ideas on *how* to approach it with the class and as a class rank the various ideas to identify an optimal one that everyone should use.

Intellectual confidence

The ability to articulate personal views based on evidence and where necessary defend them to others.

Much is said in education regarding the need for students to be self-confident, and that is of course crucial. But social confidence and intellectual confidence are different things. Being intellectually confident is about coming to a conclusion for yourself and then feeling confident enough to defend it. Much of school education is about learning new information and concepts, but the higher level activity is around making sense of those ideas and concepts. Again, some children have a home advantage in this respect and this needs to be recognised when supporting those who do not have this benefit. It is possible and desirable to build this capability in all students – but the school may have a greater role to play with some students than with others.

> Walking down the road near my house I encountered a pre-school child with her mother. The child spotted a puddle, let go of her mother's hand and ran through the puddle in her canvas shoes. The mother did not immediately reprimand her. Instead she bent down to the level of the child and said, 'Wiggle your toes and tell me how that feels'. Aha! I thought, that is an academic family. Right from the start this child is being asked to justify and articulate. They are likely to be negotiating everything from choices in the supermarket to times for bed. Consequently, by the time they start school this aspect of their development is already well advanced, they are intellectually confident and this will continue to be nurtured at home as well as at school.

Deliberately creating cognitive conflict is a useful way to help students start to hold a position and defend it. Positioning two opposing arguments and asking students to defend one or the other or perhaps giving students a choice in what or how they do something and then asking them to give reasons for their selection helps to develop intellectual confidence. Naturally, some subjects and topics lend themselves particularly well to this kind of activity, especially moral dilemmas or historical viewpoints, but all subjects can make use of this approach and with great results. And of course other techniques such as Philosophy for Children (P4C) can provide a structured way of developing this characteristic of intellectual confidence.

Linking

This section of six characteristics is about linking learning episodes and creating what Jerome Bruner calls schema (in Boswell, 1967). This is the ability to see learning as part of a larger scheme as opposed to a series of single events. It is central to constructionist theory, which assumes that education is the process of individuals constructing understanding and meaning. In school, this linking can be actively encouraged by making sure that learning objectives are not set in isolation, but wherever possible by drawing links and connections for the student. Again, some students are more naturally attracted to thinking in this way and it helps them to make rapid and secure progress in their learning. It often also reduces the amount of time they need to spend revising, for example, because their knowledge is more secure. But it is also possible to teach or train people to do this.

Generalisation

> *The ability to see how what is happening in a particular instance could be extrapolated to other similar situations.*

In an advanced cognitive performance environment people tend to be continually concerned with whether ideas or concepts have a universal applicability. It makes life easier if the same rule always applies. The English language, for example, is frustrating for learners because its grammatical rules are not universal. There are exceptions to the rule. Nevertheless, the rule applies in most cases. Asking students to think about whether what they are learning might be universally applicable helps them to group new learning in a way that will make it manageable. This type of activity can cause amusement when thinking about the result of improbable generalisations, but that in itself is useful because it makes the learning event more memorable.

Connection finding

> *The ability to use connections from past experiences to seek possible generalisations.*

Connection finding could be said to be a prelude to generalisation. Seeking connections is the start of making sense of new knowledge and information. It is very straightforward to make this a part of the teaching repertoire and can be part of the dialogue with students from an early age.

Many students are held back in their learning because they are seeking an instant, overarching framework inside which they can put their new piece of knowledge. Encouraging them to draw connections between past and present work enables them to begin to build towards that bigger picture.

Students experience a lot of satisfaction when they can see links between one piece of learning and another and this serves to increase motivation. It can be further enhanced by rewarding students for making connections and especially for making less obvious ones, for example, linking from one subject domain to another and thinking in a multidisciplinary way. Asking students if they can see a connection is a useful trigger for this.

'Big picture' thinking

> *The ability to work with big ideas and holistic concepts.*

A key characteristic of students labelled as gifted is the ability to see the significance of what they are learning and how it connects to the wider world. For many students, gifted or not, the relevance of learning is a key motivating factor and serves to enhance interest and commitment. And 'big picture' thinking encourages the development of both connection finding and generalisation. Yet much of the curricula and teaching does not attempt to position learning in this way, but rather strives to break it down into bite-sized chunks and to introduce each new piece of learning as a separate item.

A productive way to encourage 'big picture' thinking is to frame learning as contributing to big issues or dilemmas and to start new topics with a big question. At the secondary level this may be something general, such as: 'How important is "place" in novels?' This is a good way into any novel in which place is important and also allows for a wider discussion around how novels are constructed.

Coates and Wilson (2003) used this approach in their work on primary science and found that the outcomes were surprising both in terms of the children's misunderstandings and also in their ability to think with sophistication and clarity. They began their discussions with children using big questions such as the following.

- I planted a tree in my garden 4 years ago. Now it weighs 250 kg more. Where did the 250 kg come from?
- Is it true that large penguins stay warmer than small penguins?
- How will the water supply be managed on a journey to Mars, which takes 3 years?
- Why don't Australians drop off the Earth?

Some students will become engaged with a subject only if they can see the purpose of engagement, and for many exam results are not, in themselves, sufficient purpose. For these students, showing how today's learning fits into the bigger picture is crucial and they like to know what the syllabus is for the year or the topic for the term and how that will be broken down. This gives them greater control and allows them to be more autonomous. For all other students it may not be so crucial to their motivation but it is a crucial part of operating at an advanced level.

Abstraction

The ability to move from concrete to abstract thought very quickly.

It is often assumed that the most able students are those who can operate most effectively in abstract domains. It is true that being able to operate in the abstract is critical to some forms of advanced learning, but few of us operate entirely in the abstract.

Many teaching and learning theories exploit the links between concrete and abstract thinking and try to introduce children to both, for example, the Montessori method at the nursery level. Research shows that presenting knowledge in both concrete and abstract terms is far more powerful than doing either in isolation (Pashler *et al.*, 2007). This is because most of us prefer to start with the concrete and move to the abstract.

However, too much time spent on the concrete can be counterproductive. Sometimes educational theories have suggested that children are unable to deal with abstract ideas until they reach certain ages. While this might be true in some cases, it is not universally true.

> A conversation with a 5-year-old about addition resulted in his explaining that he could count the pictures of trees together in each of the circles and add them together to reach a total but it would be much easier if he just had the numbers rather than having to add the trees up first! He was already working in the abstract and was puzzled by the attempts to make the task more concrete. So encouraging progression to the abstract at whatever speed is possible is the way forward rather than being held back by notions of what children can do at certain ages.

Many researchers have looked at how people operate in the concrete and the abstract and some have added additional stages. Kolb (1984), for example, believes learners perceive and process information in a continuum from concrete experience, reflective observation, abstract conceptualisation to active experimentation.

1   **Concrete experience**: being involved in a new experience.
2   **Reflective observation**: watching others or developing observations about one's own experience.
3   **Abstract conceptualisation**: creating theories to explain observations.
4   **Active experimentation**: using theories to solve problems, make decisions.

On a practical level it is probably helpful to see the concrete as being generally preliminary to the abstract, but the speed at which we move between the two can vary not just from child to child but also from domain to domain within the same child. A visual child may be able to easily imagine the impact of changes to décor, while a linguistic one may see patterns in poetry. In reaching for advanced performance, the rule should be to actively encourage the move to the abstract but not push for an unrealistic pace.

Imagination

> *The ability to represent the problem and its categorisation in relation to more extensive and interconnected prior knowledge.*

Imagination is readily found in all young children, but like other characteristics it can be developed and enhanced. Imaginative play is valuable and helps children to make sense of their world. Howard Gardner believes each child, by the age of 7, has developed a capital of creativity upon which they subsequently draw throughout their adult lives, although this well of creativity can be topped up throughout life. The richer the initial capital, the more easily creativity flows. So early years are vital in building learning capability for the future. This kind of imaginative play is more familiar in some cultures than others, but it is worth developing whatever the cultural norms.

Imagination is often seen as a part of creativity and involving the generation of ideas or producing things and transforming them into something of value. It often involves being inventive, ingenious, innovative and entrepreneurial.

Not everyone thinks they are imaginative, but imagination can be nurtured and encouraged in school. Education Scotland (www.journeytoexcellence.org.uk/index) suggests some practical steps for encouraging creative and imaginative thinking as follows.

- Overcoming the perception that 'I am not creative'.
- Expecting the unexpected.
- Having fun playing with ideas.
- Practising not knowing or tolerating ambiguity.
- Being curious.
- Facing your fears.
- Talking to people about ideas along the way.
- Being proactive and going for it.

Seeing alternative perspectives

The ability to take on the views of others and deal with complexity and ambiguity.

For many students, seeing alternative perspectives can be a challenge. Much schooling is focused on 'getting it right' and so students begin to develop the idea that everything has a single 'right' answer. Hence, if someone holds a different viewpoint, either they are wrong and you are right or they are right and you are wrong. The more firm the child is in his or her view, the less likely he or she will be to accept the views of others.

Advanced cognitive performance includes the ability to deal with complex and some-times conflicting ideas. It requires an appreciation that situations are complex and that sometimes we simply do not yet know the right answer, or that different answers may be correct in different circumstances, or that different answers may be correct depending on the outcome we want to see. Any school activities in which multiple solutions are possible are useful in developing this tolerance of ambiguity and complexity. These can happen in class or be part of competitions or enrichment activities.

Model United Nations (http://en.wikipedia.org/wiki/Model_United_Nations) is an educational diplomatic and international relations simulation that requires students to argue the viewpoint of their allocated country. It is an excellent opportunity for building this characteristic of seeing alternative perspectives. Participants in Model UN conferences are placed in committees and assigned countries to represent. They are presented with their assignments in advance, along with a topic or topics that their committee will discuss. Delegates conduct research before conferences and formulate positions they will subsequently debate with their fellow delegates in committee. At the end of a conference, the best performing delegates in each committee are sometimes recognised with awards.

Schools do offer these kinds of opportunities and they are helpful. They do, however, tend to be restricted to areas of social science, where cultural or religious backgrounds play a significant part. They can usefully be extended to controversies in other subjects such as maths or science or the performing arts.

Analysing

This set of three characteristics is about thinking logically and carefully. Advanced performers tend to be careful and logical in their approach even when being creative. An artist like Bridget Riley, for example, is both imaginative and disciplined. Her stripes and geometric forms use both design and colour with great care and logical simplicity, but this approach creates some unique and imaginative results. In reality, some of the most creative outcomes in any domain are produced when constrained by particular conventions. For example, a poem with its defined framework can sometimes convey more than free-flowing prose.

Critical or logical thinking

The ability to deduct, hypothesise, reason and seek supporting evidence.

Critical thinking is perhaps the characteristic most traditionally associated with academic success. It is defined by Michael Scriven and Richard Paul of the Critical Thinking Community (www.criticalthinking.org/pages/defining-critical-thinking/766) as follows.

> The intellectually disciplined process of actively and skilfully conceptualizing, applying, analyzing, synthesizing, and/or evaluating information gathered from, or generated by, observation, experience, reflection, reasoning, or communication, as a guide to belief and action. In its exemplary form, it is based on universal intellectual values that transcend subject matter divisions: clarity, accuracy, precision, consistency, relevance, sound evidence, good reasons, depth, breadth, and fairness.

Schools have long believed the development of critical thinking to be useful in helping students to develop their reasoning powers and to make better judgements and evaluations. In some cases, specific courses have been created to teach it as a stand-alone subject, but as Lim (2015) points out, teaching critical thinking in schools and classrooms has so far lacked a concerted focus and is unevenly applied.

Most definitions of critical thinking foreground ideas around evaluation and appraisal – the ability to critique information and assess its validity. Traditional critical thinking courses tend to focus on the teaching of logic and argumentation as the way to achieve this and can sometimes be a bit reductionist. P4C, for example, while valuable in its own way, comes in for this kind of criticism as being an example of practice of some types of critical thinking but not the full range (Murris, 2009). Teaching students how to approach a situation logically is valuable and should not be underestimated, but it is also helpful to apply that logic to social and political situations, which are not always neat and tidy. Researchers like Lim (2015) suggest that separating the abstract, rational way of looking at the world from more empathetic considerations is dangerous as it runs the risk of creating students who do not have a social conscience or a global outlook. Hence, while you may decide to teach critical thinking as a skill in its own right, in class, critical and creative thinking should not be seen as separate and opposite skills, but rather through an understanding that in viewing a problem we may sometimes need to use both skills.

In my experience, you can easily introduce critical thinking skills into normal lessons as opposed to teaching it as a separate course. They are merely a part of the ACP toolkit. The earlier you start teaching these skills, the more likely it is that students will start to use them easily and with fluency. That will help them to perform well in most school subjects and as in future life situations.

Precision

The ability to work effectively within the rules of a domain.

Benjamin Bloom (1985), in his book on developing talent in young people, suggests that development occurs in three progressive stages: the playful stage, the precision stage and the originality stage. The first of these refers to an initial interest in a domain, which you might say was 'uneducated' in that it is instinctive and does not build on the knowledge of others. By contrast, the second stage is about learning the conventions of a domain and being able to operate well within those conventions. How to add and subtract in maths. How to do calculus. How to write a sentence. How to write a novel. How to play the piano, and so on. It is when these domains are secured that one can begin to think with originality.

Schooling could be described as the location in which students learn the rules or skills in a variety of domains. They are taught systematically, and in a way deemed appropriate for the age of the student. At its best this is exactly what happens in school, but for a variety of reasons not every student learns optimally all the time. So some students move on to new work without having properly secured knowledge of the concept or skill that has already been covered, and while they may have secured sufficient knowledge or skill to pass the assessment they are often at a loss when this concept occurs later in their schooling at a more complex level. Certainly, they are not confident enough to operate with independence and so cannot bring original ideas to the fore.

All this argues for placing greater value on precision, especially precision in following the conventions or rules accurately – even when a mistake occurs in the actual execution of the task. It is useful to point out whether the rule was followed as well as whether the answer was correct. Again, this can easily be encouraged by being explicit and drawing attention to rules or conventions, making the ACP visible for the student.

Some students dislike having to work with precision. They can be careless or can be looking to do just enough to get by. High performers tend to be precise in their work and this is a discipline that comes naturally to some but needs to be encouraged and developed in others. It is a significant factor in reaching high levels of performance in most disciplines.

Complex and multi-step problem-solving

The ability to break down a task, decide on a suitable approach and then act.

The more advanced learning becomes, the more complex it tends to become. At the start, a student may be learning in quite small steps and can link each new step easily to the last one. In more advanced learning, the tasks require the use of multiple skills and may incorporate different stages and strands.

In terms of pedagogy, some teachers break down even complex tasks into bite-sized chunks to help students reach the required outcome swiftly. This kind of approach can be useful in some circumstances but is limiting when it comes to creating autonomous learners who are confident in tackling complex problems independently. It does not help students to learn how to focus on using and applying their knowledge to deal with these complex situations. Students who are taught to depend on the teacher are not well placed to tackle the unexpected question in an exam or indeed much university study. This is one reason why some students who perform well at school fail to make the transition to high performance at the university level. These are students who have been coached at school to pass the exams but have not developed the ability to think for themselves.

This argues for the use of complex and multi-step problems as part of curriculum provision and the development of requisite skills. Of course, it can be a staged process as students become increasingly more confident in dissecting and sorting information and in planning effectively. Learning how to create a plan for tackling a complex problem serves to make it manageable and realisable.

Creating

This set of five characteristics focuses on creative thinking and learning. The concept of creativity is a popular point of discussion in educational circles. Broadly speaking, it is seen as important and a good thing. Typically, Treffinger (1980) suggests that creative learning is a good thing because:

- it helps children to be more effective when we are not around;
- it creates possibilities for solving future problems that we can't even anticipate;
- it may lead to powerful consequences in our life;
- it can produce great satisfaction and joy.

Yet it is also usually assumed that schools and education systems are not good at encouraging creative thinking and indeed may even serve to suppress it. Robert Sternberg (1995) is one of many who has repeatedly suggested that most conventional schooling stifles creativity and that education constantly seeks to stifle creative ideas. He points to the ready reservoir of creative thinking in young children that is marshalled into more conventional routes through the schooling process. He does, however, go on to suggest that creative people typically find ways to subvert those institutions to promote their ideas. Many of us will be able to draw to mind particular students who have been adept in this respect! What Sternberg and others are seeking are the paths we can all take to become more creative and ways in which institutions can learn to foster creativity.

This is obviously helpful, but a significant barrier to the development of creativity is that it can mean different things to different people. For some it means being imaginative or inventive, taking risks or challenging convention. For others it is about original thinking or producing something that nobody has come up with before. Some see creativity as entirely spontaneous and others see it as the 'Aha!' moment that comes at the end of a long period leading to deep understanding. Typical definitions include the following.

> Creativity is a combination of flexibility, originality and sensitivity to ideas which enables the thinker to break away from usual sequences of thought with different and productive sequences, the result of which give satisfaction to himself and possibly to others.
>
> (Jones, 1972)

> I define creativity as the process of having original ideas that have value. Creative work in any field often passes through typical phases. Sometimes what you end up with is not what you had in mind when you started. It's a dynamic process that often involves making new connections, crossing disciplines and using metaphors and analogies. Creativity is about fresh thinking.
>
> (Robinson, 2013)

So consensus exists only in that creativity is about the creation of something – an idea or product – that is original or novel. Around the product but not the process.

Throughout my career creativity has been a topic of interest to the education world and fierce debates have ensued about the links between curricula, such as the English National Curriculum, and the development of creativity. Does it serve to enhance or suppress it? Some curricula, such as the International Baccalaureate, purport to have been designed specifically to enhance creativity, while others seek to marry creative and critical skills. Whether or not the curriculum should be designed specifically to enhance creativity, even the early researchers into creativity saw it as something that could and should be developed in schools. Guilford (1970, p. 185), who was an influential thinker in this field from the 1960s onwards, says:

> If we look to education to foster development of intellectual skills, the implications of all this should be obvious. If we want to produce skilled problem solvers, we should see that individuals encounter the experiences that will exercise the functions in all categories (of the Structure of the Intellect Model). This means attention to curriculum building so as to provide broad opportunities for different kinds of intellectual activity, while making the content seem relevant to the learners.

In the same way as programmes to develop *critical* thinking in schools have been designed, so too have programmes to develop *creative* thinking. Yet even more than with critical thinking these programmes have proved controversial. If creativity is spontaneous, can it be taught? Is the creative process something that can, or should, be assessed? Creativity tests do exist, but once again when looking for consensus this is an area where it remains elusive with a variety of conflicting viewpoints.

What seems to be more productive territory than bespoke programmes is that of creating the cultural conditions in which creative thinking is most likely to thrive, as opposed to having creative thinking lessons. This approach can be applied to any curricula, although some are more amenable than others. Of course, fostering creativity is not a topic restricted to schools. High-tech companies such as Google view the creation of creative workspace and culture as being fundamental to achieving their business aims. Creativity should be seen as vital rather than as a 'frill' if we are to create high performing people.

So in developing the ACPs, the objective of the creative characteristics is not to teach creativity as a separate subject, but rather to introduce some ideas that are universally thought to characterise creativity and to create the conditions in school that will nurture creative as well as critical thinking.

Intellectual playfulness

The ability to recognise rules and bend them to create valid but new forms.

One of the most enjoyable aspects of learning is to flaunt the conventions. Once students know what the rules are, it is possible to play with them and to be as creative as they like. A familiar example of this is the novel. In the early development of the novel the story was told chronologically. But quickly authors found that by 'playing' with chronology they could create different effects for the reader and this opened up a vast new range of possibilities.

Students in school tend to think of learning as a worthy activity with clear right and wrong answers. Sometimes they have the opportunity to adopt differing positions, for example, on moral or ethical questions, but they rarely play with ideas in their purest form. Yet almost all domains have the potential for playfulness and the results are often satisfying and sometimes amusing. Certainly, they will be memorable.

Encouraging playfulness in learning is helpful because it is creative, motivating and often not linked to convention. It may be very appealing to students with a sense of humour or to those who find traditional learning to be routine and unrewarding. In short, playfulness can serve to build stamina and this can be useful in all kinds of ways. It also helps to put the student in control of his or her own learning and makes him or her more confident as a learner.

Flexible thinking

The ability to abandon one idea for a superior one or generate multiple solutions.

Flexible thinking and fluent thinking were two of four categories identified by Guilford (1967) in his early work on creativity and then later used by Torrance in his Test for Creative Thinking (1974). These, along with originality and elaboration, can be thought of as the cornerstones of creative thinking. Flexible thinking focuses on a child's ability to adapt to new situations, improvise and change strategies to meet different types of challenges, often abandoning an initial idea in favour of a better one. This requires the ability to think about two different concepts and to think about multiple concepts simultaneously – not always a natural process, especially when learning something new.

The ability to think flexibly is a higher order cognitive skill and a key part of the toolkit for those who achieve high levels of cognitive performance. Of course, intellectual confidence is needed in order to take the risk of thinking flexibly rather than settling for the first answer and so again this skill can be nurtured. In class, it is possible to specifically ask students to create a first solution to a problem and then ask them to create a second one and decide which they then want to use as their chosen solution and why. This starts to embed the idea that flexible thinking is useful. When this concept is mature, students will recognise that whenever their first solution does not work they need to think flexibly and find a new one as opposed to giving up. Children as young as 9 years of age who have been introduced to ACPs have been noted applying this naturally in their playground games as well as in their formal learning.

Interestingly, functional Magnetic Resonance Imaging (fMRI) research has shown that specific brain regions are activated when a person engages in cognitive flexibility tasks. So in future we may learn much more about how to maximise this capability.

Fluent thinking

The ability to generate ideas.

Fluent thinking is flexible thinking's better-known cousin and relates to having lots of ideas. Most commonly, this has been incorporated into school practice through 'brainstorming' activities where students are invited to think up as many solutions as they can.

Brainstorming has been widely adopted by business as a way to generate fresh ideas and has been thoroughly researched in that context. New and more advanced versions have arisen which purport to finesse the process, such as Keeney's Decision Sciences (Keeney, 1982).

While almost all schools already use brainstorming, it is possible to explore it more fully through the business literature and learn from their extensive experience. For example, individual brainstorming as opposed to group brainstorming has some advantages. Perhaps surprisingly, it has been found to produce more – and often better – ideas than group brainstorming. Similarly, group brainstorming has traditionally been seen as helping everyone to feel that they've contributed to the solution, but it can in fact sometimes be unsatisfactory for individuals. Unusual suggestions may not be valued by the group and potentially innovative ideas may be stifled by group pressure.

For schools, there are many websites with ideas about how to generate fluent thinking at every age and for multiple purposes. The key to success is to recognise that fluency is about generating ideas, not about evaluating them. An idea that seems unlikely could contain the seed of something worthwhile. In practical terms, one could encourage fluent thinking by asking the class to generate as many solutions as possible to the problem of global warming. This could be done as a think, then pair and then share activity, with the final stage of the task moving beyond brainstorming and involving some elements of ranking or evaluation.

Originality

> *The ability to conceive something entirely new.*

This ACP is the third of Guilford's criteria. It is the crux of innovation and the most difficult to nurture in the school setting where we have 'right answers'. Unless students are actively encouraged to be original, they will keep any original ideas they have to themselves for fear of being wrong.

However, this can be overcome. Originality is perceived in many ways and is sometimes the focus of misunderstanding. It does not have to be a life-changing discovery, but instead perhaps a simple solution or new angle on an ordinary problem. At the university level, it has been identified that students think that to be original they have to develop a 'whole new way' of considering a topic, while their supervisors assume that the student understands that it is sufficient to contribute an incremental step in understanding (Phillips and Pugh, 1994) – a much less demanding requirement. In much the same way at the school level, originality as perceived by exam boards is a 'minor' as opposed to a 'major' difference from the conventional answer. Very little is truly original in the major sense, but each individual may make original discoveries of a minor kind. Encouraging the confidence to break with tradition is a valuable attribute to nurture.

Evolutionary and revolutionary thinking

> *The ability to create new ideas by building on existing ideas or diverting from them.*

Finally, this focus on the difference between a brand new idea and one that builds on existing thinking is helpful in enabling students to move away from existing ideas towards ideas of their own. Different views exist around the extent to which an individual must have mastered the rules of any domain before he or she can evolve a new or novel solution, but the encouragement to value and be unafraid of the novel idea is worth a great deal.

Realising

Realising refers to the ability to make effective use of the other characteristics in a form that best ensures high performance. One might say that these characteristics relate to 'efficient' learning.

Automaticity

The ability to use some skills with such ease that they no longer require active thinking.

This is a psychology concept that is rarely heard mentioned in schools outside the USA. Yet in its own way it is very helpful is assisting students to achieve advanced cognitive performance. At the very least, it provides students with an explanation of why it is valuable to learn and practise skills and facts to the point at which their execution does not require thought. These include any building blocks within a specific domain that are universally used. The most obvious example of this would be times tables. Some students identified in gifted cohorts have good memories and this enables them to place large amounts of material into the automaticity space, but all students can learn salient skills or information and this can be of immense value.

Automaticity is defined by Dewey (Dr Dewey at psywww@gmail.com) as the ability to do something without thinking about it. It occurs in virtually all *overlearned* behaviour: 'Overlearned behaviour is behaviour that has been practised well beyond the point of "just barely learning it" ' (www.intropsych.com/ch07_cognition/automaticity.htm).

As you execute a skilled behaviour again and again, it gradually requires less of your attention. Finally, it becomes second nature, almost like a built-in reflex. Automaticity frees up cognitive resources. If your behaviour is automatic, your mind can wander to other things, or you can devote your attention to another useful task. A good example of this is driving a car. When you start to drive you have to think consciously about each process, but with practice this becomes automatic and you can concentrate more on the road ahead.

Psychologists divide automaticity into the conscious and the unconscious, with the former being those skills which are deliberately learned and the latter being those triggered by the environment – in other words knowing that you always do 'this' when the circumstances are 'those'.

From the teaching perspective, it is not really necessary to refine the concept but it is useful to draw students' attention to the value of increasing the number of overlearned behaviours. Students brought up on a diet of social media and video games are better at this than my generation and hence it is a cognitive process to be exploited in the contemporary world. Multi-tasking requires a degree of automaticity and this is a more natural concept for students than for teachers. It also provides a language for discussing work.

Automaticity is in direct opposition to those educationalists who suggest that we no longer need to teach knowledge because we have easy and ready access to it via the internet. Automaticity theory would suggest that may be so, but having to go and look for information is a slow and time consuming business. Far better to have the frequently used material readily to hand.

Speed and accuracy

The ability to work at speed and with accuracy.

The speed of progress in terms of learning is significantly enhanced if we learn from our mistakes instead of repeating them. This may seem obvious, but some students are much more adept at this than others. In teaching self-regulation, a school needs to help students to articulate when they are self-correcting to create greater accuracy. Mistakes are good learning points and should be seen as such, as opposed to simply getting it wrong. When a child says, 'Oh, I can see where I went wrong' this is what should be applauded and encouraged. And of course by asking, 'Next time you meet something similar what will you do?'

In reality, *accuracy* is more of a factor than speed in making swift progress. In fact, children work at different speeds with some working quickly and some more slowly. It is a personality rather than a cognitive factor. What marks out high performing students is that when they make a mistake they learn from it and adjust accordingly. So over time they become increasingly accurate. Accuracy is what we should be looking to encourage.

Students who like to work at a fast speed often make many mistakes, but the successful ones correct them quickly; this 'error and then correction' process occurs very rapidly and so they move forward swiftly. It becomes an automatic process. It can create untidy work but it is ultimately very effective. Other students like to take time to consider all aspects of a solution in advance of doing the task. They think through in their mind all the possibilities that might work and reflect on their previous experience in an attempt to minimise errors. These students appear thoughtful and sometimes a bit slow! In fact, the two approaches lead to similar outcomes in terms of speed of actual *progress* but by different routes. We cannot say that one is better than the other; just that not all students, even successful ones, approach their work in the same way.

Implementing the ACPs in school: three case studies

There are many ways to implement the ACPs in school. Indeed, one of the strengths of this approach is that it allows the teacher to work in a way that suits him or her best and meets his or her professional challenges. The three case studies that follow are from three excellent but very different teachers and the ways they have chosen to embed the ACPs reflect their own teaching approach.

Case study 1: Science

As a science teacher it is very easy to get bogged down in the relentless task of covering content-packed curricula and coaching students in passing examinations. It takes courage, and an open mind, to step back and see how administering to the wider development of each student will in the long run benefit even these narrow aims.

(continued)

(continued)

Some teachers, when first faced with the terminology of HPL, balk at the number of APCs and their apparent complexity. However, I have found that if anything they have simplified my approach to planning by allowing me to start my lesson planning process on the bigger picture and the attributes I am trying to instil in students before I think about activities to 'teach' the content of the lesson.

When teaching heat transfer by convection, I used to give the usual demonstrations (convection tube, potassium permanganate in a beaker, 'mine shaft', etc.), or even the not so usual (hot air balloon) followed by a worksheet of questions. However, when I started to think about the ACPs I was trying to develop in my class, and looked into how they could be incorporated into my lesson, I found that new avenues opened themselves, which not only taught the content more effectively, but added to the general development of the child as a student. My lesson now tends to go like this:

The class enters the darkened lab with a lava lamp placed centre stage and Glenn Gould's 'Goldberg Variations' playing in the background. I gesture for the students to sit down on pre-arranged stools, but not say anything and just continue to sit and stare at the lamp in silence. I suppose this is my attempt at getting them to think about the bigger picture and prepare them for the abstraction that will follow. The time staring at the lamp (they'll do this for several minutes!) examining a phenomenon minutely before thinking about explanations is something that I would not have tried before, but has proved an essential part of this process. After a suitable time I ask them, 'What questions do they think I will ask now?' This question of course addresses a number of the ACPs I was trying to hit when planning the lesson – certainly aspects of meta-cognition as well as imagination, strategy planning and connection finding.

'Why are we doing this? How does this work? What's happening here? What is this called? What is the lamp made of? Why are we listening to this music?'!

Eventually, I steer the conversation around to convection and give them a brief explanation of it in terms of expansion and changing density. I then split them into groups and give them an A3 sheet of paper and ask them to think of and sketch other examples of convection currents (convection currents in the Earth's mantle causing plates to move, hot air balloons, wind and sea breezes, pizza ovens, hot water heating, kettle design, etc.). You obviously have to circulate at this time and in fact this is when most of the teaching is done. Get them to exchange sheets and try to fill some gaps in one another's examples. You can then follow this discussion with the usual convection demonstrations (convection tube, ventilation shaft, $KMnO_3$ in beaker, etc.).

The crux is to test the students' understanding, and there is no better way to do this than using a 'What if . . . ?' scenario, which, while it is a technique I used before my introduction to HPL, is a perfect match for my desire to use the students' intellectual playfulness to assess their understanding. I issue groups of students (or individually if you prefer) with blank newspaper front pages with the headline 'Convection stops!' The scenario is that all convection currents have suddenly stopped and students have to consider the consequences for everyday life and the long-term survival of human life. Sections of the blank newspaper front page have titles like 'Our kitchen correspondent reports' and 'Our science correspondent contemplates the long-term effect', etc. Students then have to fill in the blank spaces.

I like to give them homework to explain convection to their imaginary 8-year-old cousin Harry using 50 words or fewer. Again, this is a teaching technique that I have used before, but which gives a great opportunity for students to meta-cognise by changing the form of information (in this case simplifying vocabulary used in class).

In conclusion, thinking about the ACPs I want to address in a lesson has reinvigorated my teaching in every aspect, while at the same time deepening my students' understanding of the most complex areas in Science. **Simon Porter**

Case study 2: English

Our English department is privileged in many respects: a strong team; small class sizes; motivated, well behaved students. However, GCSE data analyses frequently found 'bunching' around the B/A grade area with noticeably fewer As and A*s. More of a concern was that students would rarely cite English as their favourite subject and did not share their teachers' enthusiasm for literature. As a department, we were keen to use the introduction of High Performance Learning as an opportunity to consider what the barriers to excellence and high levels of engagement were in our classes.

We began by considering exactly what might be holding students back. We explored the threshold concepts of our subject: what must be mastered in order to feel confidence and truly succeed. Written accuracy was not considered the most pressing issue; students enjoyed lessons with a grammar focus and were generally very coherent writers. It was felt that the fundamental area of weakness was students' level of engagement with texts. Following the introduction of a Reading Challenge in KS3, we discovered that many students were voracious readers, almost at a competitive rate. However, when asked to discuss their responses to themes, styles and writers' intentions, they could provide only brief responses. Our students could recall facts from texts and produce lengthy essays that were essentially narrative in their approach, but they struggled to reach the deeper meaning of texts. Traditional approaches, such as teachers asking carefully considered questions and modelling the process of deconstruction for students, seemed to be rendering them passive, waiting for the 'right' answers to be revealed.

High Performance Learning had been introduced to the whole school at the start of the year and students seemed comfortable identifying which VAAs were being developed within a lesson. We started the process of enabling students to be more intellectually confident by discussing some of the Advanced Cognitive Performance characteristics, in particular Abstraction. We discussed reading as an imaginative process. As this was a difficult concept, it was helpful to encourage students to think of their own metaphors to describe mining literature for deeper meaning, like peeling layers of an onion, and language being like an iceberg. We showed James Deary's TedTalk on the abundance of metaphors in our lives to dispel the myth that only writers can conjure them up. An amusing approach to illustrating this is for students to try to speak or even write without using metaphors while others keep a tally!

(continued)

(continued)

The next step in approaching close textual analysis was to resist the temptation of eclipsing the text with context, which is immutable and so often far outside students' experience that the gap becomes difficult to fill. In order to develop their strategy planning skills, we asked students to think of an effective approach for analysing any text. They created a series of Questions for Close Reading, such as 'What is the writer's purpose?', 'What are the implications of a particular word or phrase?', 'What assumptions is the reader making?'. At this stage, they were not required to answer the questions themselves. This was to encourage them to take risks without fear of failure. They also created a series of Depth and Complexity Tasks that could be handed out at random to groups to tackle. These tasks included looking for patterns in syntax, identifying unanswered questions and looking for references to the senses. Approaches such as these enabled students to look deeply but not broadly, to examine a condensed section of text, as a group, rather than ingest it whole.

In order to add authenticity to the process and to allow the teacher to step aside as the guru of literary analyses, students were introduced to accessible authors whose literary criticism works are genuinely entertaining in themselves, such as Terry Eagleton and Edward Hirsh. We encouraged them to, as Hirsh describes, see that 'reading poetry is an adventure in renewal, a creative act, a perpetual beginning, a rebirth of wonder'. We challenged them to disagree and hold evidence-based debates on ideas raised in published essays. In turn, they wrote letters to academics challenging their interpretations. This ignited enthusiasm and an emerging belief in the validity of their interpretations.

In order to develop our readers as writers, they wrote companion pieces, parodies, contemporary interpretations and commentaries as the writers themselves. This led to a much deeper appreciation of genre forms. It was evident how impressed they had become by an art form they had undervalued, perhaps because of its abundance, in the way that one might be when watching a talented dancer or musician who performs effortlessly.

The next stage was to tackle the style and content of their written responses. Over the years, trends have attempted to provide a blueprint for literary analysis, from PQC (Point, Quote, Comment) to TIQA (Topic, Idea, Quote, Analysis). These formulas were efficient in providing an overview and essays were coherent but depth of analysis was too often absent. In order to access the complexities of a text, we used a technique we called 'Dynamic Paragraphing'. The model is built upon the foundation of key terms such as the writer 'implies' or 'suggests' in order to pick out detail, then encourages students to extend their ideas by starting the next sentence with 'furthermore' and 'in addition'. Finally, intellectual playfulness was exercised by starting the final sentence with the language of possibility, such as 'perhaps', 'might' and 'possibly'. The most successful way to introduce, refine and rehearse this technique was by collaborative writing. The improvement in the precision, quality and academic confidence of their work was significant.

There is no doubt that making the ACPs explicit empowered students and transformed the way students approach literary analysis. Teachers planned for opportunities to explore the connotations of and the skills associated with advanced cognitive performance, and, in doing so, students felt supported and motivated by their quest for an enriched appreciation of literature. **Clare Leech**

Case study 3: Sixth form maths

An introduction of HPL into mainstream teaching takes a bit of time and a clear understanding from the teacher and his or her students but the benefits are considerable. I always try to move a few steps ahead of what the curriculum is requiring in order to introduce some totally new yet solvable mathematical problems. These out-of-the-box problems to be solved are also a part of regular assessment such as tests or homework. Quite often, they also explore some cross-curricular applications of mathematics in other areas of knowledge. At some point I even think of going one step further by setting a take-home test or exam for which students are encouraged to work collaboratively together for a week in an attempt to find solutions to a unique problem (that hopefully cannot be found on the internet).

As part of the curriculum programme I deliver in class (IB Maths HL class), students are expected, in addition to tests and exams, to produce a small research work (each student does something different) that is assessed according to the criteria very much linked to VAAs and ACPs (communication, reflection, personal engagement). This requirement in itself helps with the introduction of HPL into my classroom. I am also aware that such an investigative type of assessment is already a part of or will be introduced in other mathematics curricula.

One of the questions I introduce to the students is an optimisation of a surface area or a volume of a cylindrical can. It can be done at Year 7, Year 10 or Year 12 level. The question is formulated in the following way: What is the minimum surface area of a can with a given volume or what is the maximum volume produced by a given surface area? The latter problem would probably be easier to introduce in Year 7 maths, where students would be given some paper or other material and they would have to produce the largest cylinder or a rectangular box. In Year 10, this open-ended stimulus could be set for students while working on maxima and minima of a function. However, in Year 12 (Maths SL or HL) this mathematical problem is set in order to introduce the concept of optimisation in the context of calculus and its practical application.

Prior to this investigative session, students are aware of how maxima or minima can be found using the concept of a derivative. However, the whole concept of optimisation is unknown to the students.

I ask the students to bring an empty can of cola, beer or power drink. The students measure their can and calculate its surface area (volumes are known). They calculate the dimensions of a can that would minimise the surface area and they check these theoretical results against the real dimensions. They are not in agreement. Critical and logical analysing and 'big picture' thinking must now be employed as theoretical results do not match real values. A multidimensional, additional question is also raised. This asks if theory should be matching reality. Perhaps this mismatch is intentional and has a non-mathematical reasoning behind it, for example the aesthetic appearance of a can or practical reasons such as our ability to hold this can in our hand.

Some students realise that the shape of their can is slightly different from a perfect cylinder, but in other cases (beer, power drinks) this does not explain the discrepancy. Students soon realise that thickness of the can is non-uniform and this perhaps should be considered. They try to build a mathematical model that considers different thicknesses

(continued)

(continued)

of the can. As in Karl Popper's method of scientific enquiry, students come up with newer and newer models that still differ from the real values. Each non-matching result forces students to make a better and more accurate hypothesis and to develop a more refined model. At some point, students are able to find exact theoretical thickness values that match the real dimensions of their can. Further measurement of the can confirms or rejects these findings and students keep persevering in finding a better solution.

The process leads to more fundamental questions of why there is only a minimum surface area but a maximum volume for a reversed problem. Economic and social implications follow as well. Students are now encouraged to design their own optimisation problems, for example the capacity of a football stadium.

VAAs and ACPs become a part of the assessment process whereby special criteria are designed to measure the level of reflection, collaboration, strategy planning, critical thinking and ability to generalise. These assessment criteria should provide us with important feedback about students' ability to operate outside the box.

I believe that HPL is a challenge to some teachers, particularly those operating in a well defined curriculum environment constrained by external examinations. Introducing and developing the understanding of VAAs and ACPs becomes particularly difficult for teachers who lack confidence in moving out of the box with their teaching. Implementation of HPL investigative learning also requires some careful planning, particularly when it comes to assessment. For many educators it is a paradigm shift to move from a very systematic mathematical skills acquisition type of teaching to open-ended, discovery-based learning.

However, once introduced, HPL ensures that students do learn the skills needed to be successful at their respective AP, A-level, IGCSE or IB exams. Students are thus not only well prepared for the challenges of the given curriculum, but they have also broadened their mathematical potential and improved their creative skills in mathematics.

Jacek Latkowski

References

Black, P. and William, D. (1998). Assessment in classroom learning. *Assessment in Education: Principles, Policy & Practice*, 5(1), 7–74. Published online 2006.

Bloom, B. S. (ed.) and Sosniak, L. A. (1985). *Developing Talent in Young People*. New York: Random House Publishing Group.

Boswell, J. G. (1967). Out of the Garden of Eden, with Jerome Bruner. *Journal of Teacher Education*, 18(4), 463–469.

Brown, A. L. (1978). Knowing when, where, and how to remember: A problem of metacognition. In R. Glaser (ed.), *Advances in Instructional Psychology*, vol. 1. Hillsdale: Erlbaum, pp. 77–165.

Coates, D. and Wilson, H. (2003). *Challenges in Primary Science*. London: David Fulton Publishers.

Eyre, E. (ed.) (2009). *Major Themes in Gifted and Talented Education*. London: Routledge.

Flavell, J. H. (1979). Metacognition and cognitive monitoring. *American Psychologist*, 34, 906–911.

Guilford, J. P. (1967). *The Nature of Human Intelligence*. New York: McGraw-Hill.

Guilford, J. P. (1970). Creativity: Retrospect and prospect. *Journal of Creative Behavior*, 4, 185.

Hattie, J. and Timperley, H. (2007). The power of feedback. *Review of Educational Research*, 77, 81–112.

Jarvela, S. and Jarvenoja, H. (2011). Socially constructed self-regulated learning and motivation regulation in collaborative learning groups. *Teachers College Record*, 113(2), 350–374.

Jones, T. P. (1972). *Creative Learning in Perspective*. London: University of London Press.

Keeney, R. L. (1982). Decision analysis: An overview. *Operations Research*, 30(6), 803–834.

Kolb, D. A. (1984). *Experiential Learning*. Englewood Cliffs, New Jersey: Prentice Hall.

Lim, L. (2015). Critical thinking, social education and the curriculum: Foregrounding a social and relational epistemology. *Curriculum Journal*, 26(1), 4–23. doi:10.1080/09585176.2014.975733.

Murris, K. (2009). A philosophical approach to emotions: Understanding *Love's Knowledge* through *A Frog in Love*, *Official Journal of the International Council of Philosophical Inquiry with Children*, 5(9), 5–30.

Pashler, H., Bain, P., Bottge, B., Graesser, A., Koedinger, K., McDaniel, M. and Metcalfe, J. (2007). *Organizing Instruction and Study to Improve Student Learning* (NCER 2007–2004). Washington, DC: National Center for Education Research. Available at: http://ies.ed.gov/ncee/wwc/pdf/practice-guides/20072004.pdf.

Phillips, E. M. and Pugh, D. S. (1994). *How to Get a PhD*. Maidenhead: Open University Press.

Philosophy for Children (P4C). Available at: http://www.philosophy4children.co.uk.

Robinson, K. (2013). To encourage creativity Mr Gove must understand. *The Guardian*. First published 17 May 2013, 21.59. Available at: http://www.theguardian.com/commentisfree/2013/may/17/to-encourage-creativity-mr-gove-understand.

Schunk, D. and Zimmerman, B. (2007). Influencing children's self-efficacy and self-regulation of reading and writing through modeling. *Reading & Writing Quarterly*, 23(1), 7–25.

Shayer, M. and Adey, P. S. (1993). Accelerating the development of formal thinking in Middle and High school students IV: Three years on after a two-year intervention. *Journal of Research in Science Teaching*, 30(4), 351–366.

Shore, B. M. (2000). Metacognition and flexibility: Qualitative differences in how gifted children think. In R. C. Friedman and B. M. Shore (eds), *Talents Unfolding: Cognition and Development*. Washington, DC: American Psychological Association.

Sternberg, R. J. and Lubart, T. I. (1995). *Defying the Crowd: Cultivating Creativity in a Culture of Conformity*. New York: NY Free Press.

Torrance, E. P. (1974). *The Torrance Tests of Creative Thinking – Norms – Technical Manual Research Edition – Verbal Tests*, Forms A and B – Figural Tests, Forms A and B. Chicago, IL: Scholastic Testing Service Inc.

Treffinger, D. J. (1980). *Encouraging Creative Learning for the Gifted and Talented*. Ventura, CA: Ventura County Superintendent of Schools.

Veenman, M., Elshout, J. and Busto, V. (1994). Metacognitive mediation in learning with computer-based simulations. *Computers in Human Behaviour*, 10, 93–106.

Veenman, M. V. J., Van Hout-Wolters, B. and Afflerbach, P. (2006). *Metacognition and Learning: Conceptual and Methodological Considerations*. Published online 8 March 2006. Springer Science and Business Media, Inc.

Wolters, C. A. (2011). Regulation of motivation: Contextual and social aspects. *Teachers College Record*, 113(2), 265–283.

Zimmerman, B. (2008). Investigating self-regulation and motivation: Historical background, methodological developments, and future prospects. *American Educational Research Journal*, 45(1), 166–183.

Chapter 5

The Values, Attitudes and Attributes (VAAs)

The Values, Attitudes and Attributes (VAAs) work in conjunction with the ACPs and together they enable students to progress towards advanced cognitive performance. The VAAs are the learner *behaviours* that students need to exhibit. They create the thinking, caring person, not just what my colleague Dr Susan Leyden called 'brains on legs' – or indeed a test-passing machine – but rather a well rounded individual able to thrive in the adult world as well as in the school setting.

Much interest has been shown in recent years in this question of the characteristics schools should be developing alongside academic scores. In the USA this is termed creating 'college-ready' students, while the International Baccalaureate calls it the 'learner profile'. In England we have seen this idea come through in vocational competencies and the work of such programmes as SEAL (Social and Emotional Aspects of Learning).

Values education is not a new idea. Neil Hawkes (2013), the founder of Values Based Education, has been working in this field for over 20 years and it could also be said that most faith-based schools place values at the heart of their mission. What is different now is that in a more global and multicultural world the need for a strong moral compass is more pressing than ever and education is seen as having an explicit role to play in helping to create the citizens of the future. McDonough and Feinberg (2003) describe this as considering how best to redefine and reassert the core values of liberal democracy in the light of new circumstances and conflicts created by multicultural democracies.

In England, 'character education' has become a vehicle through which to build values. Building on the concept of 'grit' as defined by US-based Paul Tough in his book *How Children Succeed* (2012), the idea of character has become fashionable in education in the twenty-first century and recognises the links between the behaviours and attitudes a child needs to exhibit in their learning and eventual academic success.

The definition from the Jubilee Centre at Birmingham University (www.jubileecentre. ac.uk/432/character-education) adopted by the English Department for Education suggests:

> Character is a set of personal traits that produce specific moral emotions, inform motivation and guide conduct. Character education is an umbrella term for all explicit and implicit educational activities that help young people develop positive personal strengths called virtues.

So some of the interest in values comes from a sociological concern, but other concerns are also being expressed in relation to education. There is a real shift in thinking about the purposes of education, in the possibilities created by education and in the demands now placed upon education.

Employers, for example, are interested in 'attitudes', which one might call 'work readiness', as opposed to, or in addition to, 'college readiness'. These include values but are also related to what has previously been referred to as 'soft skills', such as those listed by the UK National Careers Service (www.nationalcareersservice.direct.gov.uk):

- Communication
- Decision-making
- Showing commitment
- Flexibility
- Time management
- Leadership skills
- Creativity and problem-solving skills
- Being a team player
- Accepting responsibility
- Ability to work under pressure.

In England, John Cridland, Director General of the Confederation of British Industry (CBI), is quoted in the 2014 CBI/Pearson Education and Skills Survey (CBI/Pearson, 2015) thus:

> We need a system that better reflects how well a school's culture nurtures the behaviours and attitudes young people will need. Success should be measured by where young people go once they have left school or college, not on exam results alone.

Certainly, research into what employers look for when recruiting would suggest that attitudes are important. The global recruitment company Reed found in their 2011 survey (www.ReedGlobal.com) that 96 per cent of employers would hire someone who did not have a complete set of skills but displayed the right attitude in preference to an applicant with the perfect skills but who lacked the right mindset. They were primarily seeking commitment, honesty, trustworthiness, adaptability, accountability and loyalty.

The VAAs listed as part of the High Performance Learning framework are designed to help students to be both college-ready and employment-ready but also 'life-ready' and well prepared for a successful future. In schools already using existing values or character frameworks it is not necessary to move from one to another. The major advantage of the HPL set is that the progression routes have been created for each VAA, so enabling students and teachers to see the development of VAAs as being comparable to academic development. The High Performance Learning VAA groups are Empathic, Agile and Hard-working.

Empathetic

This set of three VAAs looks at the way in which individuals approach working alone and with others to achieve strong outcomes.

Collaborative

The ability to seek out opportunities to receive responses to your work; to present your own views and ideas clearly and concisely; to listen to the views of others; be willing and able to work in teams; to assume a variety of roles and be able to evaluate your own ideas and contributions.

The ability to collaborate is a key skill in life. For some it is a natural and straightforward one and for others less so. It is not necessary for students to prefer collaboration as a way of working, but they do have to be able to collaborate when required. Hence, ensuring that each student can achieve this is important and schools should exhibit a proactive approach to the development of this skill.

Schools frequently talk about the need to collaborate and often ask students to work in groups or teams. This is not always as collaborative as might be assumed. Without a framework for co-operative learning, group work can be a quite negative experience, with dominant members of the group holding sway and others feeling isolated or unvalued.

For novice collaborators it is helpful to teach and practise collaborative skills. Careful listening, for example, or presentation skills can help students to operate more effectively in this respect. Particular techniques such as coaching can also help to build collaborative capability, and of course rewarding examples of good collaboration helps to raise esteem within the classroom. Many schemes and programmes exist that can be used in the classroom to foster collaboration and can be found on Continuing Professional Development websites; for example, Concept to classroom (www.thirteen.org/edonline/concept2class/coopcollab).

It is worth noting, however, that the ability to work alone and independently is also a valuable skill, and hence collaborative work should not be the default position. Where this default operates, it proves a hostile environment for the child who finds it difficult to work with others either because of shyness, lack of self-confidence, through strong belief in his or her own views or through an inability to align his or her concentration levels with those of others. These kinds of students need to be helped to collaborate, but often our best work comes when we can work in our preferred way, and for some that means through collaboration and for others through working alone.

Concerned for society

The ability to know the contribution you can make to society to the benefit of those less fortunate; to demonstrate citizenship and a sense of community ethos and recognise differences as well as similarities between people and peoples; be aware of your own and others' cultural heritage and be sensitive to the ethical and moral issues raised by your studies.

This concern is at the heart of work on values education and is an important if sometimes difficult area to nurture in school. Certainly, it cannot be the responsibility of one teacher alone but rather must be a culture or ethos that pervades the school.

For those of us who have worked in international schools where seventy or eighty different nationalities are working alongside each other every day the idea of cultural difference is an obvious reality. Students learn other languages and customs from their friends as well as through formal schooling, and different ideas and expectations are the norm. Yet even in these environments teachers sometimes fail to make maximum use of the opportunity in curriculum terms. Individual students come from different traditions and it is immensely enriching when discussing curriculum in art, music, literature, science, history and so on to capitalise on this richness of viewpoints. It is of course also challenging for the teacher to have to chair and manage differing or opposing opinions, but this is exactly where tolerance and good citizenship development occurs. Pride in your background should not mean intolerance of the backgrounds of others.

More difficult still is to develop these characteristics in either monocultural environments or in binary environments in which the home view prevails and other perspectives may be seen as alien and hostile. Yet it is equally important that students develop a more global viewpoint because the unfamiliar or unknown is often threatening, and when threatened, individuals often cease to be open-minded. Here, the school needs to be even more proactive and careful in its approach and may be looking to actively partner with, for example, a school in another country.

Of course, differences in society are not restricted to cultural differences. For most students, their first experiences of 'difference' may be socio-economic if some of their school friends come from less or more wealthy families than their own. Again, the school can do much to foster tolerance, care for others and the benefits of recognising the community or communities of which we are a part. For older students, research studies provide conclusive evidence that socio-economic disadvantage places a burden on the individual in terms of aspiration and ambition but that does not in itself prohibit healthy approaches to citizenship. Views of socio-economic disadvantage are relative, not universal. Many schools in disadvantaged areas in England have recognised that by supporting schools in, for example, rural Africa, their own students have the opportunity to care for those less fortunate than themselves rather than always being in the cared-for, dependent, category.

Ample opportunity exists for the nurturing of concern for society, both through specific schemes and more generally through the day-to-day life of the school. The British Council helps UK schools to link to schools overseas and technology makes it possible for such links to be both viable and enduring. This topic has never been more important, and for a student to be successful and high performing in adult life they need to develop their own moral compass which helps them to take a leadership role in society.

Confident

The ability to develop a belief in your knowledge, understanding and action; recognise when you need to change your beliefs based upon additional information or the arguments of others; deal with new challenges and situations, including when this places you under stress.

Students who perform highly tend to be intellectually confident and are often also socially confident. Success breeds confidence and while we can all probably think of the individual 'geek' who lacks confidence in social situations, it tends to be the exception as opposed to the rule. In reality, the stereotypical view of the antisocial geek is just a myth. Most academically successful people are also socially at ease.

Intellectual confidence is, however, something quite different. Intellectual confidence, which is also sometimes called 'academic self-concept', refers to a student's self-belief that he or she has the capacity to succeed academically. This is a student's self-evaluation of his or her own academic worth or capability. It is not static and can be improved. Researchers such as Herb Marsh (University of Oxford) have suggested that there is a reciprocal effect between a child's self-concept and their educational outcomes. Success, educationally, will lead to intellectual confidence, which in turn leads to further academic achievement. So provided that a student can experience some initial success – and that it can be reinforced from time to time – confidence should follow.

The culture of the school – and indeed the home – can do much to enhance or to undermine intellectual confidence. Schools that adopt a constructionist approach, with an emphasis on success and next steps in learning, are likely to help a student to feel more confident than those that focus on whether the student is 'good' or 'weak' academically. Equally, it is helpful for parents to know that sympathising with a child struggling with maths by saying that they too found maths hard, and it runs in the family, can serve to confirm helplessness in the child rather than instil confidence. The conversation at home or in school should acknowledge that the child is struggling *now*, but reinforce the idea that this is just a stage and that he or she will eventually be able to succeed.

Au and colleagues (2010) in their interesting longitudinal research into secondary school success found that although previous attainment was the strongest predictor of eventual success, intellectual self-concept was the next most significant factor. 'The greater the students see their achievement as a function of others and not themselves (e.g. effort), then the higher the later levels of learned hopelessness, learning difficulties and lower self-esteem.'

The most successful high performing students remain confident that they have the capability to achieve even when they are not currently being successful. This enhances their willingness to tackle difficult or unfamiliar work and to take risks. Hence, building this intellectual confidence is a vital skill in the high performance toolkit, and hence one which schools need to take seriously. Many students do not feel intellectually confident when facing new work, but using the ACPs really can help to empower students in their learning and increase their confidence.

Interestingly, praise and encouragement can have downsides if used inappropriately. Brad Bushman of Ohio State University found that parents who tell their children that they are more special than others do not in fact enhance their child's social or intellectual confidence or self-esteem. Indeed, 'overvaluing' practices may inadvertently raise levels of narcissism. There is a growing body of research led by Kamins and Dweck (1999) exploring the perils of praise and recognising the importance of praise of 'effort' as opposed to 'ability'.

Agile

This set of four attitudes relates to the desire to learn and being prepared to use multiple approaches in order to achieve good outcomes. They are dispositions that enable students to become more autonomous and to contribute well in school and in life.

Enquiring

The ability to be curious; be willing to work alone; be proactive; keen to learn; show enterprise and independent thought; challenge assumptions and require evidence for assertions; actively control your own learning; move on from the absorption of knowledge and procedures to developing your own views and solutions.

Curiosity is at the heart of learning and those with an insatiable curiosity are often those who are willing to work hardest to achieve the mastery that will enable them to make sense of the world. So they will practise and strive and this in turn results in high performance, so encouraging curiosity from the earliest age is useful. Again, a large canon of research exists that explores the links between curiosity and educational attainment and it is sufficiently compelling to suggest that encouraging the development of curiosity is a school essential. Curiosity is a key motivator.

Debate does exist about the extent to which curiosity in individuals is innate, but like all other characteristics which may have an element of predisposition curiosity seems to be teachable. Engel (2011) found that children who were encouraged by their teacher to be curious in class became (maybe unsurprisingly) more curious. What this shows is that, as with other behaviours, if they are encouraged and valued in class, they will be developed. Some might argue that certain curricular approaches aid curiosity and indeed that some testing regimes inhibit it, but educators should always be looking to institute a pedagogy that foregrounds curiosity regardless of a syllabus of assessment regime and this is as true for secondary (high) school students as it is for primary (elementary) learners.

Unfortunately, the track record for schools in terms of nurturing curiosity is not good. Engel (2015) in her latest book suggests that curiosity is a robust trait in early childhood but becomes more fragile over time, and is shaped by experiences with parents, teachers, peers and the learning environment. She stresses the centrality of language and question-asking as crucial tools for expressing curiosity and also points out that although curiosity leads to knowledge, it can stir up trouble, and schools often have an incentive to quash it and instead promote compliance.

Two key factors in the development of curiosity are parents and early years' provision. Parents of very successful adults, especially scientists, have been found to have actively fostered and encouraged curiosity and wonder, especially in the natural world. By contrast, early years of course provide the first opportunity for formal education to instil this characteristic. For children whose own families have not fostered curiosity – for whatever reason – this is a vital opportunity to instil that sense of potential in learning.

Creative and enterprising

The ability to be open-minded and flexible in your thought processes; demonstrate a willingness to innovate and invent new and multiple solutions to a problem or situation; adapt your approach according to need; surprise and show originality in your work, so developing a personal style; be resourceful when presented with challenging tasks and problems, using your initiative to find solutions.

Curiosity in turn leads to creative and enterprising thinking. Exploration of ideas or concepts inevitably leads to new thoughts and hypotheses. In school, an overly rigid curriculum or approach to teaching can quash creativity and enterprise in students. If you want to encourage these you must create the time for exploration and willingness to deal with setbacks on the road to success. Being creative and enterprising is not a tidy or linear process and progress on the journey can be hard to recognise and certainly hard to assess.

One reason that 'freedom to roam' in education is so beneficial is because it allows students to feel for themselves the satisfaction which comes with a discovery. Talking to the press following the award of his Nobel Prize for Economics in 2010 (Nordstrom, 2010),

Dale Mortensen stressed the importance of experiencing 'aha' moments: 'I think anyone who's engaged in creative life – whether they're a scientist, economist, writer or artist – has many "aha" moments, many moments to discovery, otherwise they wouldn't be doing it.'

These kinds of moments do not have to be original on an epic scale, but they do have to serve as a conquest for the individual no matter what age or discipline.

In some schools, enterprise has sometimes been seen as developing only outside normal class activity, through enrichment or extra-curricular activities – or indeed gifted and talented programmes. In reality, every student's curriculum should comprise both formal and these more informal learning opportunities and enterprise should be a factor in both. Enrichment and non-timetabled sessions do provide exemplary conditions for creating greater freedoms and time to explore in depth, but students should learn that using enterprise and creativity is valuable in all types of learning, even the most constrained.

In England, enterprise has become associated with activities set up in school to create workplace scenarios. For example, the Young Enterprise Scheme (www.young-enterprise.org.uk) argues that: 'An excessively narrow focus on academic skills and exams risks sidelining other approaches to learning and can fail to give young people the employability skills they need to succeed in the world of work.'

While this and other similar schemes are undeniably of value in creating opportunities to practise enterprising thinking and creativity, it would be wrong to suggest that academic work does not require enterprising and creative thought, or indeed that other approaches to learning (whatever those may be) do not contain a cognitive element. This bifurcation is unhelpful. It is more helpful to think of enterprise as a possible dimension in all learning as opposed to being restricted to workplace learning.

Open-minded

The ability to take an objective view of different ideas and beliefs; become more receptive to other ideas and beliefs based on the arguments of others; change ideas, should there be compelling evidence to do so.

For many students, open-mindedness can be a struggle. This is especially so for those with strong views and opinions, but also for those with few views of their own who are looking to others for guidance as to the 'right' view or opinion on any given matter. The curriculum can be used to create opportunities for the development of individual viewpoints and this is indeed a key cognitive skill. But the curriculum can also be used to position opposing ideas or multiple ideas, and this can help students move beyond merely holding an opinion towards changing or adjusting their opinion in the light of new information. So in practical terms you could, for example, set a task for which certain information is made available and that might lead students to an obvious viewpoint, but then drip-feed additional information which may change that view. This kind of activity works well in a variety of domains from forensic science type tasks in which clues are made available, to moral or social questions to which evidence on why views are held may be added.

As we learn more about the development of the brain, we are starting to understand that this question of open-mindedness may have a neurological, developmental aspect. Sarah Jayne Blakemore (Blakemore and Robbins, 2012) suggests in her latest work that decision-making in adolescence may be particularly modulated by emotion and social factors, for example, when adolescents are with peers or in other affective ('hot') contexts. So retaining open-mindedness in adolescence may turn out to be more difficult than in later or earlier life. Certainly in the social context of school these kinds of findings may be pertinent.

Nonetheless, a school with an open-minded and tolerant ethos is best placed to foster that in its own students; and helping students to acquire the skills which enable them to critique the viewpoint of others without its appearing to be criticism of the person is a useful life skill.

Risk-taking

> The ability to demonstrate confidence; experiment with novel ideas and effects; speculate willingly; work in unfamiliar contexts; avoid coming to premature conclusions; tolerate uncertainty.

Intellectual risk-taking is again recognised as a valuable skill for students. But again, schools do not have a good track record of providing the requisite opportunities for nurturing this vital skill.

Students take risks because they sense the possibility of a favourable outcome. Risk-taking – as distinct from risk – involves decision-making that considers insuring oneself against possible loss (Trimpop, 1994). So it is a considered approach as opposed to an unthinking or rash act.

Students who are intellectually confident are also more likely to be risk-takers. This is because when they do not know the answer for certain, they are more confident in creating a hypothesis about suitable answers rather than feeling helpless. Intellectual risk-takers have been shown to be particularly successful in tests. Once again, this is a trait that comes more naturally to some, but can be developed in others.

It has been argued that the High Stakes testing regimes adopted by the UK in the 1990s and subsequently adopted internationally have been a prime reason for the reduction in opportunities for students to experience risk-taking. In a culture in which teachers are measured on the success of their students in public tests the temptation to 'teach to the test' is very strong. It drives an incremental approach to education, breaking down all learning opportunities into bite-sized chunks and measuring progress on each separate piece. This is fundamentally at odds with the more holistic High Performance Learning approach which foregrounds building capability as the best preparation for test success.

Of course, teaching students how to make decisions that insure them from possible loss is valuable. While risk-taking in exams is a high stakes activity, risk-taking in class is only as high stakes as the teacher makes it. If the school encourages calculated risk-taking, then students will become more proficient in it and more likely to reach the highest levels.

Hard-working

Hard work comprises practice, perseverance and resilience. Concentration and practice are required not just in pursuit of understanding but also in refining or improving. Persistence or the ability to keep practising is also critical, as is the stamina to keep going and the resilience to dig deep even when it seems as if the task is impossible. All these characteristics could be said to be personality based, with some individuals inherently more predisposed to them than others. However, the way in which learning is presented and rewarded can substantially increase willingness to concentrate and persevere.

Practice

> *The ability to train and prepare through repetition of the same processes in order to become more proficient.*

Daniel Levitin (2006) in his research has established that mastery in any domain, be it cognitive, sporting or artistic, does not come easily – it requires immense practice.

> The emerging picture from such articles is that *10,000 hours* of practice is required to achieve the level of mastery associated with being a world-class expert. It seems it takes the brain this long to assimilate all it needs to know for true mastery.

The consequence of this is that children will only become proficient in the required ACP characteristics if they are a feature of their daily educational diet throughout their schooling, and if they themselves recognise them and know that they are the key to success. In addition, the school needs to celebrate progress in these dimensions just as much as it celebrates conventional academic progress, as they are the building blocks to eventual academic success.

Perseverance

> *The ability to keep going and not give up; encounter obstacles and difficulties but never give up; persist in effort; work diligently and work systematically; do not be satisfied until high quality, appropriate precision and the desired outcome are achieved.*

Arguably, the single most important characteristic in advanced cognitive performance is the ability to persevere. Perseverance is the willingness to keep going for the long haul and also to cope with setbacks and discouraging experiences. Of course, it is difficult to be categorical about why some students will persevere more than others, but again, although this may include an element of predisposition it can certainly be fostered. Much earlier in my career I looked at concentration in the nursery and was surprised to find that contrary to the wisdom of the time, a minority of children were capable of concentrating on a single task for up to 45 minutes. This ability is atypical but would undoubtedly be useful during formal education and indeed in later life. These children would be among the most likely to be identified as gifted.

We know that this factor of perseverance is important in long-term success. Many studies have pointed to it and many successful individuals have indicated the same.

Jalil and Boujettif (2005), in their research into Nobel Laureates, found this perseverance was a factor that the Laureates thought had been instrumental in their success.

> Steve Chu (Physics 2007): I either learned or inherited the desire to stick with something until I got the answer. Also, I love to work with my hands, building things such as model airplanes, playing with Erector Sets, chemistry sets, and so on. These activities developed mechanical intuition and spatial skills.
>
> Robert Mundell (Economics 1999): I put myself through college and that created habits of work and concentration that were a great help to me in later years.

How schools can build this persistence is being taken more seriously internationally. The inclusion of perseverance in the US Common Core Standards has led to increased attention being given to this characteristic, with practical ideas on fostering perseverance emerging from researchers in a range of topics (Bray, 2014). Equally, John C. Fischetti (2014) cites this as one of the five trends affecting education across the world. Education seems to have woken up to the importance of perseverance. The task now is to help students make that a reality. For them perseverance is linked to interest, to motivation, to attainable goals and to intellectual confidence. It is important to recognise the value of hard work, but without belief in one's own ability to succeed it becomes a demoralising experience.

Resilience

The ability to overcome setbacks; remain confident, focused, flexible and optimistic; help others to move forward in the face of adversity.

Martin and Marsh (2003) suggest that the answer to academic success lies not just in the ability to practise but in resilience. They refer to Howard and Johnson's (1999) description of resilience as being the process of, capacity for, or outcome of, successful adaptation despite challenging or threatening circumstances and suggest that in the academic context it is defined as students' ability to deal effectively with academic setbacks, stress and study pressure.

As in adult life, this question of resilience cannot be separated from self-concept or from ideas such as 'grit', and so on. We know that students need to be self-confident if they are to be resilient in the face of adversity. We also know from the life stories of successful adults that their lives were rarely problem-free and that the ability to bounce back was a critical factor in their eventual success.

In adult leadership programmes, considerable emphasis is given to recognising the need for resilience and to identifying personal mechanisms that will help individuals to strengthen it. Similarly, students need to understand that setbacks are a natural part of progress, and that developing the ability to be resilient is critical to long-term success. The school context is not always best suited to building resilience, especially in the secondary (high) school. Much of school is about achieving at a set time and in a set way. So students learn that initial failure is irretrievable.

Resilience is about bouncing back when meeting setbacks and so it is particularly important that schools: (a) make students aware that setbacks are natural and commonplace, and that it is not the setback that is important but rather how you deal with it; and (b) are explicit about the ways in which second chances are made available.

Rewarding achievement the second time around as being as good as or better than initial effortless success is critical to building self-belief.

Martin and coworkers (2010) refer to this ability to bounce back as academic buoyancy. They have identified five motivational predictors of academic buoyancy in the high school context. These are referred to as the 5Cs of academic buoyancy: confidence (self-efficacy), co-ordination (planning), commitment (persistence), composure (low anxiety) and control (low uncertain control). They provide a useful framework for discussing resilience with students and helping them to become more resilient.

Advanced cognitive performance is the journey towards mastery of a subject or topic or skill. Such activity is not easily acquired and schooling at its best recognises that at every stage students will need to strive to conquer difficult or perplexing concepts. Much of the literature about successful people does indicate that inventor Thomas A. Edison's famous comment that 'genius is 1 per cent inspiration, 99 per cent perspiration' is correct and that no-one holds a special magic ticket that will guarantee achievement at advanced levels. It is in no small part the result of hard work.

References

Au, R. C. P., Watkins, D. A. and Hattie, J. A. C. (2010). Academic risk factors and deficits of learned hopelessness: A longitudinal study of Hong Kong secondary school students. *Educational Psychology*, 30(2), 125–138. Available at: http://doi.org/10.1080/01443410903476400.

Blakemore, S. J. and Robbins, T. W. (2012). Decision-making in the adolescent brain. *Nature Neuroscience*, 15, 1184–1191. doi:10.1038/nn.3177. Published online 28 August 2012.

Bray, W. (2014). Fostering perseverance: Inspiring students to be 'doers of hard things'. *Teaching Children Mathematics*, 21(1), 5–7.

CBI/Pearson (2015). *Gateway to Growth*. London: Pearson.

Engel, S. (2011). Children's need to know: Curiosity in schools. *Harvard Educational Review*, 81(4), 625–645.

Engel, S. (2015). *The Hungry Mind: The Origins of Curiosity in Childhood*. Boston: Harvard University Press.

Fischetti, J. C. (2014). Issues in education: The rubber duckies are here – Five trends affecting public education around the world. *Childhood Education*, 90(4), 316–318.

Hawkes, N. (2013). *From My Heart: Transforming Lives Through Values*. London: Crown House.

Howard, S. and Johnson, B. (1999). Tracking student resilience. *Childhood Australia*, 24(3), 14–23.

Jalil, A. and Boujettif, M. (2005). Some characteristics of Nobel Laureates. *Creativity Research Journal*, 17(2–3), 265–272.

Kamins, M. L. and Dweck, C. S. (1999). Person versus process, praise and criticism: Implications for contingent self-worth and coping. *Developmental Psychology*, 35(3), 835–847.

Levitin, D. J. (2006). *This is Your Brain on Music: From 'Neurons' to 'Nirvana'*. London: Atlantic Books.

Martin, J. and Marsh, H. W. (2003). *Academic Resilience and the Four Cs: Confidence, Control, Composure, and Commitment*. Paper presented at NZARE Conference 2003. Available at: http://www.aare.edu.au/data/publications/2003/mar03770.pdf.

Martin, A. J., Colmar, S. H., Davey, L. A. and Marsh, H. W. (2010). Longitudinal modelling of academic buoyancy and motivation: Do the '5Cs' hold up over time? *British Journal of Educational Psychology*, 80, 473–496.

McDonough, K. and Feinberg, W. (2003). *Citizenship and Education in Liberal-democratic Societies*. Oxford: Oxford University Press.

Nordstrom, L. (2010). Nobel science laureates name creativity, patience, humour as prize-winning traits. Associated Press, 7 December. Available at: http://www.thestar.com/news/world/2010/12/07/nobel_science_laureates_name_creativity_patience_humour_as_prizewinning_traits.html.

Tough, P. (2012). *How Children Succeed: Grit, Curiosity, and the Hidden Power of Character*. New York: Houghton Mifflin Harcourt.

Trimpop, R. R. (1994). *The Psychology of Risk-taking Behaviour*. Amsterdam: North-Holland.

Chapter 6

Creating and leading a High Performance Learning school

High Performance Learning is an approach that is best applied to schools that are already performing well and looking to move from good to world class. It assumes that the senior leadership of the school is already good and is capable not only of driving through requirements outlined by others, but also of building on these to create its own unique educational vision and of driving that forward with year-on-year improvements in terms of success. It also assumes that the majority of teaching is good and the workforce supportive. Of course, no school is perfect but these are the features of 'good' schools and hence the starting point for introducing the advanced pedagogy that creates world class schools.

Overall methodology

High Performance Learning theory outlines a set of ideas and principles that transforms the outcomes of schools by ensuring that many more students achieve highly. Through the framework it identifies the complete set of component parts that are needed to make this a reality. It is systematic and can be used over time. What it does not do is put these into a step-by-step programme. This is deliberate. Each school is a unique institution and the best schools exploit that unique context in the creation of their own educational vision and supporting protocols. These schools are at the point of development that Hargreaves calls 'The Fourth Way', whereby the post-standardisation agenda calls for the school to play a greater role in defining its own way forward (Hargreaves and Shirley, 2009). High Performance Learning gives schools the freedom to innovate and create within a well thought through framework.

So a High Performance Learning school will have its own vision, which is shaped and underpinned by High Performance Learning theory. In a similar way, the precise nature of the learning opportunities it offers and the support frameworks it creates will reflect the community, people and needs of the school while adhering to the High Performance Learning principles, as opposed to adopting High Performance Learning as an off-the-shelf programme. This requires good leadership at all levels and a professionalised workforce that relishes educational problem-solving and can use the High Performance Learning framework to create educational solutions for the school.

A successful High Performance Learning school is a place of scholarship that exudes interest and celebration of all types of learning. It is purposeful but not pressured and creates time for fun. Its students are successful. They all feel that, given a commitment to study, they are set fair for success. It is a confident school, but always looking to do that little bit better. Staff enjoy their work and even though they have the odd frustrating day, overall they can see progress in their students and their own professional life.

Cumulative effects over time

Important in High Performance Learning is the recognition that learning is a carefully orchestrated journey, and so the longer a student is exposed to the High Performance Learning framework in school the greater the effects are likely to be.

In a through-school environment in which all age groups use this same approach to pedagogy the effects have been greatest, but even when a student is moving from school to school, if both schools are using this framework then dips in performance are likely to be minimised. This is particularly significant for groups of schools such as Academy chains, whose sites may be different for primary (elementary) and secondary (high) schools, but whose pedagogy can be the same. Indeed, having an overarching pedagogy can create a really effective way to build professional learning communities among staff. Using High Performance Learning in Nord Anglia Education's thirty international schools in eleven different countries allowed us to have a shared language and expectations around pedagogy, and that in turn allowed us to showcase and celebrate practice designed in one school and see it admired and replicated in another. Overall this helped to magnify the effects.

Of course, it is not essential for a student to experience High Performance Learning throughout his or her entire education for it to be beneficial. That is merely the optimal situation. If students are taught this way in one school, it will equip them with the tools for learning that will enhance their capability to learn wherever they find themselves. So, if taught this way in primary school they will use it in secondary school, and if taught it in secondary school they will use it in university and the workplace. What you are doing is equipping students for life. It is just that the more they have formal opportunities to develop the ACPs and VAAs, the better their chance of reaching proficiency and eventually high levels of academic performance.

Accountability

The overall key performance measure for High Performance Learning is student performance in school, in public examinations and in post-school destinations (where relevant). However, within the school it is also useful to consider a range of sub-factors that contribute to those milestones.

The first group of sub-factors consists of those traditionally associated with well managed schools, i.e. those of careful planning, strong systems and processes, financial probity and quality personnel at all levels. These are key factors that enable any organisation to run well on a day-to-day basis and to achieve its ambitions. The second group of factors consists of the objectives that relate to the effective implementation of the High Performance Learning philosophy. These include the overall vision of student success, flexible mindset, advanced learning opportunities, support structures, implementation of ACPs and VAAs and reward structures.

A significant feature of High Performance Learning is that if a school believes that all students are capable of achieving highly, the number who achieve this will: (a) be the key metric of measurement, and (b) should increase year on year as the school becomes more adept at creating high performers.

This means a move away from looking at 'strong' and 'weak' cohorts and instead look-ing at the effectiveness of the organisation in nurturing high performance in students. The significance of this change cannot be overestimated. It is fundamental and affects every aspect of the life of the school. The accountability lies with the school as an organisation and its effectiveness as an organisation in realising its core task. Just as in a hospital the propor-tion of patients surviving critical surgery is not measured in terms of how sick the patient was on arrival, but instead how effective the hospital was in treating that illness. Survival rates are expected to be universally high or improving year on year as the hospital gets better at its job. That is what a world class school expects of itself too.

In addition, individual departments and teachers will continue to measure the mile-stones, such as the value that is added to the performance of individuals because it is success in each individual journey that creates overall school success. However, they will extend these progress measures and link them to the gap between current performance and high performance. Hence assessments will routinely consider:

- previous performance;
- progress from previous performance; and
- distance from 'high' performance.

This provides the data to enable effective interventions at the individual level and stu-dent tracking. It should be noted here that the acquisition of cognitive skills and learner behaviours is not a neat and tidy linear process, so although summative assessment is important it should not dictate the overall pedagogy. High Performance Learning is a curriculum-led approach, which leads to strong summative assessment outcomes rather than an assessment-led approach in which the teacher is teaching to the test. As the old adage goes, weighing the pig frequently does not make it get fatter.

Teachers are at the front line of securing better learning outcomes, but High Performance Learning does not dictate the process that teachers must use in their individual lessons to achieve it. There is no teaching template for embedding the ACPs and VAAs. The starting point is an assumption that the teaching professionals in the school are competent and can select the best ways of working in their subject or phase to embed the High Performance approach, while being cognisant of the relevant factors and possible pitfalls. Striving to improve teaching quality is fundamental but this is a collaborative activity, starting from a strong base, with teachers owning responsibility for improving their own practice and meas-uring the effectiveness of their work in terms of the outcomes for their students. Schools that are heavily managed as opposed to led are often intolerant of variety in approach and indiscriminate in their interventions, when it is precisely this flexibility that enables world class performance. Teachers must be allowed to read the situation, diagnose the best ways forward and adapt their practice accordingly. They must move beyond seeing teaching as a set of defined management practices that they must demonstrate indiscriminately.

Assessment of teaching quality should be rigorous, but it is likely to be largely peer to peer with occasional benchmarking by senior teams and systematic coaching of weak teachers to develop them. Just as High Performance Learning assumes that all students can achieve highly, and systematically builds a structure around them to achieve this, so too can this methodology be applied to teachers and teaching. Hence, accountability and development of teachers should follow the same pattern of high expectations and capability building. Only when student outcomes are being seriously affected should teacher accountability be more draconian in approach. A school with a culture of mistrust of its teachers will be unable to develop the culture needed to create a sense of intellectual confidence and well-being in its students.

Student-centred leadership: creating the school's vision

Unsurprisingly for an approach that is built on enhancing student capability, the concept of what Viviane Robinson calls student-centred leadership is the most effective overall leadership approach (Robinson and Hargreaves, 2011). As she points out, a well organised school is an essential precondition for learning, but it is not sufficient. Equally, happy staff and parents are important but do not necessarily translate into benefits for the children. So, in an approach such as High Performance Learning where we are looking to systematically build a structure that provides optimal learning opportunities and the support structures that encourage personal motivation, placing students at the centre of the school's thinking and leadership is the best route to success (see Figure 6.1).

Research over many years on effective school leadership is unanimous in pointing to the need for the school head teachers (principals) to be the proactive leaders of learning (Fullan, 2002; Leone 2009; Newton and Wallin, 2013; Hallinger and Lu, 2014). In the UK this was an idea supported by the English National College for School Leadership through its training programmes, and in the USA this change from the principal as primarily manager-administrator to leader of curriculum improvement (Ediger, 2014) has also taken hold. It has also been identified as a differentiating factor in the top systems in Asia (Harris, 2014) and so might be described as a global concept.

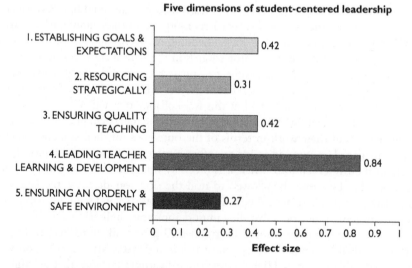

Five dimensions of student-centered leadership

Figure 6.1 Student-centred leadership

Source: Robinson and Hargreaves, 2011.

So what does it mean for a principal to lead learning in a school? In my experience, some school principals are more passionate and informed about learning than others and hence better able to scope out a unique way forward. One category of senior leaders and principals is of those embarked on an educational mission to provide outstanding education for the students in their care. It is their primary concern and all other factors are secondary. Others are driven more by affirmation of their effectiveness as managers and take great pride in being able to meet external requirements. When these are focused on standards they are passionate about them, but often less so about the process that leads to them. They are strongly goal focused.

For the first group, knowledge and understanding of teaching and learning are a continuing, collaborative quest which they are seen to lead, and they create a culture in which professionalism is valued and recruit staff who are similarly driven. Standards are important, but they are an outcome and the result of carefully planned, effective education. Good management is seen as important too, because it supports and enables better student learning. High Performance Learning is best suited to this group. Leaders of High Performance Learning need to dare to be inspiring and to lead their team confidently through this new exciting and challenging educational journey. They will set out the protocols and procedures, engage in the discussion and debate, but place trust in their team to convert ambition into reality.

As with any development within the school, the need for it to be school-wide and for all senior leaders to be early adopters is paramount. The senior leaders must be the advocates and ambassadors, and if that is to occur they must truly see this as game changing. To make High Performance Learning effective you need leadership from the top, from the middle and within the classroom. Everyone is a leader of learning – even the students themselves – but it is the senior leadership that must take the time to fully understand and buy in to this approach.

The overall proposition of High Performance Learning is compelling and immediately attractive to most teachers, but the implications are less attractive because it means letting go of some established and well rehearsed practices. A real danger is superficial engagement whereby the ACPs and VAAs are introduced but not used frequently enough to make the difference, or where some existing practices that pull against the High Performance Learning approach are retained and serve as a pull-back on progress; for example, traditional approaches to planning, setting or reporting. It is for this reason that when looking to become a High Performance Learning school the senior team needs to consider the best structures for implementation. High Performance Learning is a unifying focal point of effort, and acts as a clear catalyst for team spirit (Collins and Porras, 2005), but even team spirit can come under strain when movement towards the vision requires you to let go of familiar or treasured practices.

Heuristic evidence suggests that schools can be successful in introducing High Performance Learning in a wide variety of ways. They may opt to do the following.

- Take the traditional route and create a working group that plans in advance and then rolls out across the school with relevant milestones.
- Have a 'big bang' introduction and plunge in and refine as you go. This approach described in 1982 by Peters and Waterman (as cited by Michael Fullan, 2009) is a popular alternative.
- Introduce the terminology and allow staff to play with it for a while before embedding it more fully in a more structured approach.

- Set up a professionals study group to investigate how to make this work in parts of the school and then expand it.

In the end, it is up to the school to decide what usually works best in their school in terms of introducing new ideas and how best to build enthusiasm and sustain it. Each approach has strengths and weaknesses. But in education the biggest threat of all is that we have become accustomed to regular, externally demanded change requirements and hence have become cynical and well skilled at appearing to change while simultaneously neutralising change. We have also become very good at setting off but less good at maintaining and embedding over time and across changes in key personnel. Yet this is what world class schools have cracked. They are good and they stay good. Their underpinning philosophy is permanent and guides and filters all new initiatives and external demands.

Senior and middle leaders: making the vision a day-to-day reality

As the school adjusts its practice to bring it into alignment with High Performance Learning theory, senior and middle leaders are the 'engine' for change. It is the middle and senior teams which have the wide-ranging responsibilities that cover multiple classes or age groups and hence have the greatest influence. They will be the people to turn the overall strategy into day-to-day operational practice.

For this reason, they are a key stakeholder group when it comes to winning hearts and minds. However, even if they accept the new ideas in principle – and some may not – the senior and middle leaders and their teams have to fathom out what all this might look like in practice and decide on a methodology and sequencing any changes. This is not straightforward and if not handled carefully can lead to superficial results.

For example, while blanket introduction of the ACPs and VAAs is the most obvious starting point, the most thoughtful and successful schools have chosen to focus on a subset for development in the first instance. They may choose a teaching topic and use specific ACPs proactively within it, or they may decide to take a more structured approach and sequence introduction over the lifetime of the phase, with a subset developed in each year group and then additional ones added in the next year group, etc.

As with all learning initiatives the effect on student outcomes is enhanced if the approach is consistent and developmental across phases and subjects, and so this is what senior and middle leaders should be looking to achieve. As far back as 1997 (Thomas and Sammons, 1997), research was indicating that it was difficult for schools to secure consistency across subjects and within subjects over time. So this challenge should not be underestimated. However, the way to achieve this in a good school – that is looking to become world class – is not through a management approach which frequently checks on implementation in each classroom, but rather by agreeing a set of protocols and then leading the professional learning community as staff work collaboratively to agree on successful ideas and approaches in the classroom. Using the High Performance Learning framework as the base pedagogy provides a shared agenda that enables teachers to be more focused and deliberate in making changes to their practice. The frequently used approach of deciding where we are now, where we want to go to, and how we are going to get there serves to provide a simple usable structure for this.

Most importantly of all for senior and middle leaders is the need to galvanise the teaching team, prepare them for the journey, agree milestones and then celebrate success frequently and regularly.

Teachers and teaching: teachers as professionals

Advocates of the post-standardisation agenda for system development such as Michael Fullan (Fullan, 2009) suggest that it differs from the standardisation agenda in that it is more about 'mindful, deeply engaged, critical and challenging teaching and learning'. This requires excellent teachers. The High Performance Learning approach fits well within this system ambition: it assumes that teachers are broadly effective, and that the best way to further improve performance is to draw on their professional capabilities.

Teachers are professionals and how to manage professionals is a topic not restricted to education. Professionals generally are seen as highly skilled, knowledgeable and independent of mind, but also insecure and in need of a lot of reassurance if they are to maintain their motivation. This is why the traditional carrot and stick management approaches do not fit very well and do not serve to bring out the best in professionals. Overt criticism serves to make them even more insecure and they respond by being defensive or losing interest. Professionals resist direction, question authority and like to be their own boss (Davies and Garrett, 2013).

The heavy teacher accountability systems that have dominated the education space in the West in recent years have led to professionals feeling misunderstood and undervalued. The use of traditional management approaches has led to low respect for managers by professionals, whom they are likely to think of as bean counters and bureaucrats. So if senior and middle leaders in school are to be effective in managing their teaching professionals they need to establish a mandate to manage (McKenna and Maister, 2005). They need to be seen as 'first among professional equals' as well as effective managers. They need to recognise that they are working with highly talented people who know what to do and how to do it. These people need direction and steering, not carrot and stick.

Over the years, many terms have been used to describe teachers who think for themselves and are intent on continuously improving their practice. They may be termed reflective teachers, teacher researchers, practitioner researchers, etc. They tend to collaborate with others in their school and with the wider professional community and they remain fascinated and excited by their job. They often share their excitement with the students and their love of learning transmits itself to the students in their care. They include their students in their professional investigations and even encourage them to become researchers themselves (Kellett, 2005; Davies and Lewis, 2013). They are teachers who see themselves as professionals who are continually striving to improve their professional practice and achieve ever better outcomes for students.

While significant numbers of this kind of teacher are what the school needs, it cannot afford to leave the development of such professional attitudes to chance. It must be proactive and create the culture in which teacher enquiry is as firmly embedded as student enquiry. It must create an enquiry-based learning school. This is desirable for all schools, but it is essential for High Performance Learning schools because teachers need to demonstrate the Values, Attitudes and Attributes (VAAs) that they are looking to develop in their students. They need to be the role models. They must see expertise development as it relates to their profession as being reflected in their own learning journey. High Performance Learning is about lifetime success, so even though a school is focusing on the part of the journey that relates to school-aged students, this will only be authentic if the school demonstrates that those at a later stage of life are still learning and becoming increasingly expert in their chosen domains.

High Performance Learning allows teachers to be highly creative within a clearly defined but flexible framework. In this context, good teachers are truly imaginative and envision possibilities that turn the ACPs and VAAs into fascinating but demanding learning opportunities that motivate students and challenge them to reach for new levels of understanding. Having the framework as a shared agenda allows for focused experimentation alone, with others and as part of study groups, etc. It also makes an excellent focus for the use of professional learning techniques such as 'lesson study' (Dudley, 2014).

The wider school community

In a school that is underpinned by the High Performance Learning philosophy everyone is a learner and is acting in support of other learners. Whether teaching assistants or playground supervisors or school cooks, they all need to be seen to take a pride in their work and strive to achieve greater levels of expertise.

Sharing the High Performance Learning philosophy with everyone in and associated with the school is key to making it pervade the school. It is good for everyone, not just for students. Everyone needs to know that this is how the school sees student capabilities and what they are trying to achieve. It must become the lingua franca of the school. For example, a teacher who has been suggesting to a child that the problems he or she is encountering with English as a subject is not terminal but rather a stage of current performance that can be improved will not have much credibility if the teaching assistant, in trying to comfort the discouraged child, later says, 'Oh never mind, you're just not that good at English. I am sure you are good at other things.' The possibility of high performance must be a consistent message to students from everyone in the school.

More positively, team members such as teaching assistants are a critical part of the support structure and often have more one-on-one time with students than the teacher. They can use this time to good effect to offer support within the High Performance Learning framework. They can be the front line in building motivation with those who are struggling and in reinforcing the message that performance now is not an indicator of the future. The tone of their dialogue with students will be around saying 'You just need to focus on the next step and step by step you will get there. We believe in you'.

Systems and protocols

The High Performance Learning framework does not set out any specific organisational structures or protocols, but rather leaves this to the senior leaders of the school. What is important is that the existing structures and protocols that have given the school stability and enable it to work well and focus on its core business of teaching learning are well aligned to the more sophisticated objectives of the High Performance philosophy. It may be that the existing structures already work well, but even in a school with a strong focus on teaching and learning it is useful to review these to ensure full alignment. In particular, the following areas are worthy of consideration.

Teacher appraisal and performance management

A world class school needs great teaching, and good teaching should be celebrated while any underperformance needs to be remedied. In the best schools or organisations self-assessment is the first stage of any assessment of professionals. They are often very self-critical and underestimate their performance rather than overestimate it. So performance management discussions should start with the person to be assessed being encouraged to give a self-assessment and then this being calibrated by the assessor. It is just as likely that the assessor will be calibrating upwards and seeing the overall performance more positively as it is that they will be calibrating downwards. Areas for improvement should be agreed and mechanisms for that can range from working informally with others to mentorship or to specific coaching. A school should be concerned if a teacher is not able to give a self-assessment because this indicates either a lack of self-awareness or more probably a sense that the criteria for judgement are externally set and beyond their control. How would Ofsted (Office for Standards in Education) or similar external evaluators judge me as opposed to how I judge myself, given my professional expectations and external requirements? It is helpful to check that the existing performance management scheme is developmentally driven as opposed to summative because the culture set out in High Performance Learning is around flexible mindset and a belief that everyone has the capability to be a high performer. World class schools are an engine room for creating world class teachers – they do not just recruit them.

Core curriculum and assessment

The High Performance Learning approach can work with any curriculum and assessment framework. It is concerned with pedagogy rather than content. As a school moves towards embedding the High Performance Learning approach, it will need to look carefully at how best to exploit the curriculum and also consider the extent to which existing assessment arrangements are fit for purpose. Curriculum and assessment provide the backdrop for the key tenets around the provision of advanced learning opportunities and development of individuals through meaningful formative assessment. So although all curricula provide opportunities for teaching to focus on advanced learning, it is helpful to look at where the most obvious opportunities exist because they make a good starting point. Equally, to consider the extent to which assessment is a process 'done to' the student and where it enables students to be involved in assessment of their progress. Again, where this is already happening is a good starting point. It is not helpful when adopting High Performance Learning theory for the school to up-end its current practices wholesale. This distracts from the core teaching and learning, but an audit is useful because it sets out a future agenda that can be adjusted over time with clear milestones in terms of pace and nature of change.

Enrichment and extra curricula

In terms of opportunities, High Performance Learning suggests that in lessons the major adjustment is to have universally high expectations and to offer advanced learning opportunities – for example, classroom challenge – to all or as many students as possible. Teach to the top rather than the middle and also provide support to enable students to fulfil the demanding requirements. This should be the day-to-day diet for students.

However, enrichment (additional opportunities which are not part of the core syllabus) and extra-curricular activity (taught outside the normal school timetable) can provide perfect locations for advanced learning, and often in a form in which students can follow their personal interests as opposed to being engaged in compulsory activity. They are popular and motivating for students and provide something different and a new arena in which to excel. We know that high performance requires practice and often extra-curricular time is when students can practise extensively, especially in arts, sports and music. Of course, these don't have to be the only types of activity on offer. Richard Feynman loved his advanced algebra class, and chess and Latin have proved very popular extra-curricular activities in some schools. Here, parents can be useful in helping and if there is a parent who writes alternative comedy you can be sure that any class he or she offers will be oversubscribed.

In enrichment activities the topics on offer can be different from the traditional school subjects, and somehow an enrichment session on perfume making is more appealing than school chemistry. Many schools have harnessed the interest in forensic science to capture the interest of students, but equally, great scenarios using maths have been created. In schools that have instituted non-timetabled enrichment days the activities offered are interdisciplinary, develop new skills and offer a dazzling array of topics. So schools know how to do this. What High Performance Learning requires is for these activities to be seen as an ideal location for building advanced thinking through the ACPs and establishing attitudes through the VAAs.

I am not suggesting here that each activity should have to formally demonstrate their ACPs and VAAs, but rather that, for example, in the quest to create global citizens enrichment activities can play a useful part. Typically, Model United Nations (www.nmun. org) is an educational simulation and an academic competition in which students learn about diplomacy and international relations. Many schools participate in this and it helps to develop a range of ACPs and VAAs. Similarly, if a school is working with a partner school in another country, enrichment time often offers the chance for more meaningful work and hence the development of relevant VAAs.

The key message is that enrichment and extra-curricular activity provide a top location for developing advanced thinking and good learner behaviours, so they should not be seen as an add-on but rather as a critical part of the school offer and valued accordingly. An audit of the current range and whether it could/should be more fully exploited is useful.

Rewards

Rewards systems make explicit to students what it is that the school values and hence they provide a vehicle for encouraging the behaviours you want to see. Different schools handle this in different ways and that is appropriate. There are many ways to reward and encourage students and staff. In thinking about High Performance Learning it is useful to reflect on the existing systems. Do they reflect the philosophy? It is worth considering both their nature and their frequency.

Some schools actively reward demonstration of the ACPs and VAAs. In the nursery class this might involve being allowed to wear the persistence medal (such as a lanyard) for the morning if you have shown 'perseverance' and have your photo taken on a tablet and sent home, and in secondary school it might be a certificate presented to the student. There are no right answers here but there are endless creative opportunities.

Student grouping

It is not possible to adopt High Performance Learning without inevitably reaching a point where the question of ability grouping comes to the fore. Teachers will point out that while they may believe that everyone can achieve high performance eventually, many of them are not there now, so surely we need to differentiate.

Student grouping or setting is a difficult topic at the best of times because the evidence is conflicting. We know that the students like to be taught in sets (Hallam and Ireson, 2006), but often feel they should be in a higher set (Hallam and Ireson, 2007) where the work would be more demanding – so suggesting that students' expectations of themselves are higher than those of their teachers. We know that the top sets are often not composed of the most intellectually able, but rather the most compliant and school enthusiastic (Hallam and Ireson, 2007) – so may be inequitable; and that ability grouping influences the expectations of pupils, teachers and parents regarding pupil prospects (Gamoran, 1986; Kerckhoff, 1986) – so may lower expectations in some instances. We also know that students in the second set are as capable of advanced performance as those in the top set – so are disadvantaged if they do not have access.

The UK Department for Education review of pupil grouping in 2005 indicates that:

> Pupil grouping is often presented as a polemical debate between setting and mixed-ability teaching. The research evidence suggests that schools show a much wider range of grouping practices that vary with age of pupils (especially at transition into secondary schools) and curricular area. In addition, consideration of pupil grouping should include a variety of within-class groupings, and organisational and within-class grouping for both social and academic purposes. In order to explain evidence of associations between grouping, learning and social behaviour, the review suggests that school, department and classroom decisions regarding pupil grouping are more complex than a reflection of 'seating' arrangements.
>
> (Kutnick *et al.*, 2005)

A recent small study looking at pupil grouping in New Zealand (Hornby *et al.*, 2011) found that approximately 75 per cent of schools used ability grouping, but principals did not see substantial benefits from this. Their decision to use ability grouping was not evidence-based but rather based on the personal views of management, or possibly they were just following custom and practice in other schools. So, in considering the best way forward to create High Performance Learning, it is not so much a question of whether 'to group or not to group' but rather the importance of having a well thought-through approach to this. If you group, will it still allow everyone to aim for high performance? The second set may be going to the same destination as the top set, but perhaps by way of a different route. What is important is that no ceilings are placed on student achievement as a result of the school's structures, and at the same time any grouping arrangements must be manageable from the teaching perspective.

Timetable and teaching time

In developing the ACPs and VAAs, some teaching and learning approaches are especially helpful. The overall High Performance Learning framework points to enquiry-based learning, expertise development, feedback and practice. While these can be accomplished in any situation, it is worth taking a closer look at the timetable in terms of whether the allocated slots are of sufficient duration to allow for in-depth study and investigations. If all lessons are short, then the opportunities for extended work are diminished. Of course, some activities are better suited to short lessons, so it is the overall package that is important.

As with other forms of management, there is no optimal template for either volume of teaching time or for length of lessons or for duration of units of study. Hattie (2008) in his list of influences on student achievement did not find any of these factors to be particularly significant, but common sense suggests that flexibility and a thoughtful approach to the creation of learning opportunities are bound to be beneficial.

However, High Performance Learning is about having high expectations, and so it is likely that more will be expected of students than has traditionally been the case. Lessons will not be pressured but they will be pacy. The school needs to ensure that in comparison with the average school it offers more in terms of:

- breadth,
- depth, and
- pace.

Mental health and well-being of students

High Performance Learning has universally high expectations of what students can achieve academically. Consequently, a potential risk must be that students feel under pressure to achieve and then become stressed. This should not be so. We know from the extensive body of research into gifted students that placing pressure on students does not necessarily lead to better academic outcomes and indeed can lead to their becoming increasingly risk-averse. We also know that boredom and low expectations can result in misbehaviour and disengagement. So the key is to get the balance right and to help each individual to feel that he or she is making progress towards high performance. Teaching to the test in England has resulted in increased levels of stress in some students, prompting the *Times Educational Supplement* (Maddern, 2014) to suggest that: 'Stress at school is the biggest contributor to depression, self-harm and attempted suicide among young people, according to research published today.'

The question of student well-being should be at the heart of any world class school. As far back as 1943, Maslow established that unless our basic needs are secured we are unable to deal with higher level functioning. Good schools should be healthy places for students in terms both of physical and mental well-being, and the adoption of High Performance Learning should serve to enhance rather than diminish this.

The idea of what Tracy Cross (Cross, 2015) calls 'honoring the active role that an individual plays in her or his psychological development' is important in a High Performance Learning school. He suggests that this might be best secured in a 'bill of rights' for students (see Table 6.1).

Table 6.1 Student entitlement

Students should have the right to:

- be treated as a valuable member of the school environment;
- receive consistent encouraging messages about their abilities and achievement without being subjected to undue pressure, ridicule, guilt and the like;
- have access to a rigorous, complex and challenging curriculum;
- have access to well trained teachers who will use best practices in pedagogy including gifted education pedagogy;
- accelerate through the school's curriculum at an appropriate pace;
- attend a school that is safe physically, socially, emotionally and intellectually;
- spend some time during the school day with intellectual peers;
- make some choices about what they study and how they pursue it;
- have the opportunity to use library resources without having to pay extra for them;
- attend a school that is free of anti-intellectualism;
- practice time in their passion areas as a means to reach their potential as a student;
- use technology to its fullest extent in pursuing their passions;
- make friends beyond their same-age classmates typically imposed by schools;
- have the opportunity to make friends around their passion areas;
- not be required to spend time engaged in busywork;
- demonstrate their knowledge and skills on pretests, before instruction on any particular topic is provided;
- have both proactive and therapeutic counselling services;
- be taught how to be a culturally competent person;
- have the opportunity to pursue extra-curricular activities without having to forego academic pursuits;
- attend a school that is free from political influences that affect the quality of education available to the students.

Source: Cross, 2015.

References

Collins, J. C. and Porras, J. I. (2005). *Built to Last: Successful Habits of Visionary Companies*. London: Random House Business Books.

Cross, T. L. (2015). Social emotional needs. *Gifted Child Today*, 38(2), 128–129. doi:10.1177/1076217515569278.

Davies, G. J. and Garrett, G. (2013). *Herding Professional Cats: Being Advice to Aspiring Leaders in the Professions*. Axminster: Triarchy Press.

Davies, O. and Lewis, A. (2013). Children as researchers: An appreciative inquiry with primary-aged children to improve 'Talking and Listening' activities in their class. *Educational & Child Psychology*, 30(4), 59–74.

Dudley, P. (2014). *Lesson Study: Professional Learning for our Time*. London: Routledge.

Ediger, M. (2014). The changing role of the school principal. *College Student Journal*, 48(2), 265–267.

Fullan, M. G. (2002). The change leader. *Educational Leadership*, 59(8), 16–20.

Fullan, M. G. (2009). Leadership development: The larger context. *Educational Leadership*, 67(2), 45–49.

Gamoran, A. (1986). Instructional and institutional effects of ability grouping. *Sociology of Education*, 59, 185–198.

Hallam, S. and Ireson, J. (2006). Secondary school pupils' preferences for different types of structured grouping practices. *British Educational Research Journal*, 32(4), 583–599.

Hallam, S. and Ireson, J. (2007). Secondary school pupils' satisfaction with their ability grouping placements. *British Educational Research Journal*, 33(1), 27–45. doi:10.1080/01411920601104342.

Hallinger, P. and Lu, J. (2014). Modelling the effects of principal leadership and school capacity on teacher professional learning in Hong Kong primary schools. *School Leadership & Management* (formerly *School Organisation*), 34(5), 481–501. doi:10.1080/13632434.2014.938039.

Hargreaves, A. P. and Shirley, D. (2009). *The Fourth Way: The Inspiring Future for Educational Change*. Thousand Oaks, CA: Corwin Press.

Harris, A., Jones, M., Adams, D., Perera, C. and Sharma, S. (2014). Asia–Pacific education researcher. *Springer Science and Business Media B.V.*, 23(4), 861–869.

Hattie, J. (2008). *Visible Learning*. London: Routledge.

Hornby, G., Witte, C. and Mitchell, D. (2011). Policies and practices of ability grouping in New Zealand intermediate schools. *Support for Learning*, 26(3), 92–96. doi:10.1111/j.1467-9604.2011.01485.x.

Kellett, Mary (2005). *Children as Active Researchers: A New Research Paradigm for the 21st Century?* United Kingdom: ESRC. Available at: http://oro.open.ac.uk.

Kerckhoff, A. (1986). Effects of ability grouping in British secondary schools. *American Sociological Review*, 51, 842–858.

Kutnick, P., Sebba, J., Blatchford, P., Galton, M. and Thorp, J. (2005). *The Effects of Pupil Grouping: Literature Review*. Research Report 688. London: DfES.

Leone, S., Warnimont, C. and Zimmerman, J. (2009). New roles for the principal of the future. *American Secondary Education*, 37(2), 86–96.

Maddern, K. (2014). School stress to blame for student depression. *TES Magazine*, 5 July 2013. Updated 12 May 2014. Available at: http://www.tes.co.uk/article.aspx?storycode=6342512.

Maslow. A. H. (1943). A theory of human motivation. *Psychological Review*, 50, 370–396.

McKenna, P. J. and Maister, D. H. (2005). *First Among Equals*. New York: Free Press.

Newton, P. and Wallin, D. (2013). The teaching principal: An untenable position or a promising model? *Alberta Journal of Educational Research*, 59(1), 1–17.

Robinson, V. and Hargreaves, A. (2011). *Student Centred Leadership*. Chichester: John Wiley and Sons.

Sammons, P., Thomas, S. and Mortimore, P. (1997). *Forging Links: Effective Schools and Effective Departments*. London: Paul Chapman Publishing Ltd.

Chapter 7

The role of parents, universities and employers

Parents, universities and employers all have a role to play in enabling, promoting and shaping the delivery of High Performance Learning. High Performance Learning is deliberately designed to create learners who are academically successful in school and who exhibit the characteristics that will enable them to do well in life and in the workplace. It is a developmental approach in which each learner is an individual on a journey to success. All these learners will encounter setbacks and problems, and for some these will be greater or more enduring than for others. But the High Performance Learning approach is about optimising the circumstances in which a child is likely to succeed and removing individual barriers that stop him or her from doing so. Crucially, it is about believing that they can.

Schools are a key context for the development of the necessary Advanced Cognitive Performance characteristics (ACPs) and the Values, Attitudes and Attributes (VAAs), but learning is not restricted to schools. It occurs outside of school as well as inside school, and so many people have a role as educators of children and young people.

Parents

Children do better at school when the school and their parents are working in harmony and sending a consistent message. In a High Performance Learning school parents can amplify the effect of High Performance Learning by playing their own part in helping their child to develop and practise the ACPs and VAAs. Of course, this should not be a chore or create stress for the child, but rather be a natural part of day-to-day activity. If it becomes too overt and makes the child feel that home is just another school, then it ceases to be of value.

Parents can play a significant role in helping their child to reach high levels of cognitive performance. This is not a question of pushing and insisting, but rather one of coaxing and sometimes coaching. Many parents are trying to do this already, either unconsciously or consciously. The High Performance Learning vocabulary helps parents to be clearer about how they can support their child and why developing the relevant skills and attributes can be important in school and in life.

High Performance Learning sends a set of messages to parents about how they can best support their child to become a high performer through day-to-day life at home.

Expect your child to have the ability to achieve highly and show him/her that you have confidence in him/her

Most parents hope that their child will do well at school, but at the outset they are usually unsure about how education will develop for him or her. If their child appears to be ahead of his or her friends in terms of speaking and numbers in preschool or indeed has learned to read early, most parents think this is a signal that their child is bright and will do well at school. Equally, if their child has delayed speech or is very active and not interested in cognitive learning activities, they often start formal schooling with a worry that all may not be well in the long run.

It is important that from the outset parents demonstrate confidence in their child and in their abilities to do well. Children develop at different rates and what is happening now is not necessarily a strong indicator of the future. Parents need to demonstrate a sense of belief that will help the child believe in himself or herself. They need to encourage and support even when it is a struggle to conquer the task. It is tempting with young children – or even older ones – to take over, as it is the quickest way to get the task done, but doing your child's homework or tying their shoelaces for him or her is not an effective way to help him or her develop. Patience and time are what is needed.

It is also worth remembering that some children are sensitive and remember the thoughtless comment that suggests they are 'no good at . . .' or 'will never be a mathematician', etc. These light-hearted comments may not seem so light-hearted to the child. They may shape his or her self-concept. So care is needed from the parent, but also in helping the child to see that sometimes remarks made are not terminal: 'I was angry/busy/tired when I said that and didn't mean it.'

Equally, praise itself has some perils. If parents praise their child for being clever or smart, then it has been shown that this makes them think they will do well even if they don't try (Dweck, 2007). What works is for parents to praise their child for their efforts because this encourages a 'growth' mindset. So 'well done for having a go or sticking at that' or 'you are so much better at that than you used to be' or 'do you remember when you could only . . .', etc.

These kinds of ideas are often seen as important in early childhood when attitudes and self-concept is being developed, but they are equally important throughout life. Adolescence, for example, is an important time when young people are seeking their own identity and can be very self-critical and lacking in confidence or seeking perfection. Parents should continue to express confidence and praise effort, whatever the age of the child. It is especially important to support in this way when a young person fails to achieve something they really want, for example, the place at university they wanted or the grades at school that will enable them to take up their chosen career. It is here that belief becomes critical. If you don't succeed the first time, then it is disappointing, but many people have had to come back and try again in order to succeed and praising that persistence and resilience is key to helping your child overcome setbacks.

Encourage curiosity

Parents are often the first people to switch their child on to learning. Many of the most successful people had parents who encouraged them to be curious, to question and to feel a sense of wonder about the world around them. Of course, some children are naturally curious, but even for them curiosity can be enhanced and affirmed and for others it can be developed.

Posing questions is at the heart of creating curiosity (see table 7.2). If you actively encourage your child to be curious and to ask questions about how things work, about why the sky is blue, about why some numbers are in a pattern and some are not, and why the story ends that way or indeed about any day-to-day issues, then they will start to question for themselves. There is much research to suggest that high achievement and curiosity are strongly linked. This may be because being curious means you are more likely to find out about things for yourself and to read around the subject as well as follow the taught course. You may also want to practise until you improve.

Help your child develop empathy

Empathy is the ability to understand and share the feelings of others. It is not an inherited characteristic. We are not born empathetic (Coutinho *et al.*, 2014). We learn how to become empathetic, and this skill – like all others – is acquired more easily by some than others. Yet it is important. Children who are empathic tend to do better in school, in social situations and in their adult careers. Children and teenagers who are the most skilled in empathy are viewed as leaders by their peers (Kutner, 2013).

Kutner suggests that we can start teaching empathy from an early age. Young children frequently make inappropriate comments, especially about anyone or anything that is different. When a child is about 5-years-old, it is possible to teach empathy by talking about hypothetical problems. 'How would you feel if someone took a toy away from you?' or 'How would your friend feel if someone took a toy away from him?' By the time a child is aged 8, he or she can grapple with more complex moral decisions and appreciate that someone else's feelings may be different from his or her own.

Table 7.1 Questions to trigger discussion with children

1   Questions that encourage meta-thinking, linking, analysing:

- Why ...?
- How do you know that ...?
- What evidence do you have ...?
- What is similar? Different?
- What happens when ...?
- What do the experts say about ...?

2   Questions that encourage creativity, agility:

- What if ...?
- In how many ways ...?
- What would it look/be/sound like if you created ...?
- Imagine if you ...
- Create a hypothesis about _____ and see what happens.

3   Questions/prompts that encourage empathy and self-awareness:

- How do you feel, believe, think about _____ and why?
- How would you decide about ...?
- Which would you prefer _____ , _____ or _____ and what are your reasons?

Of course, empathy is a life skill and we can continue to develop it over time. It helps with collaboration because it is easier to collaborate with someone if you are thinking about them and trying to see their point of view as well as your own. In the home, opportunities to teach empathy are abundant and range from tolerance of siblings to why sending a thank-you note to an ageing aunt or not picking flowers in other people's gardens is good. Again, this topic tends to be thought about at an early age but is equally relevant in adolescence. Helping your child to understand the point of view of others is helping to develop a key skill.

Empathy is also important in understanding difference and in creating tolerance. It enables children to feel more at ease with their community and makes it possible to talk to even young children about why some people look or do things in a way that is different from us. This in itself helps children to become more open-minded, not just in respect of other people, but in their thinking generally. This in turn helps them to be more creative and innovative. They can 'think outside the box'.

Talk and read with your child and help them connect up ideas

The higher order thinking in the ACPs is all about being able to manipulate knowledge and make sense of it. As a parent you can help your child do this better by doing some simple things that encourage reflection and connecting of knowledge. Mostly you want to get your child to hold an opinion and to be able to defend it based on evidence as to why they think that way.

For young children, stories are a shared activity with parents in many households and provide a great way to generate discussion and debate. 'Book Talk' refers to discussing the book, not just reading it, and can involve you in asking why characters did what they did, and whether your child would do the same. Also, whether it would be possible to have the same book set in a different place and whether a different ending would be better. This can be a lot of fun and can be playful, with 'silly' ideas or suggestions as well as clever ones. Equally, you can use your own family experiences to encourage generalisation – would it always be like this if we did this? The natural world also provides a wonderful context for looking at same and different.

Later reading may mean online and press or social media, where again the opportunities to express a view or opinion are manifold. Encouraging the vocal and sometimes seemingly unreasonable adolescent to express a view is far superior to his or her becoming isolated and distanced. As they develop their own views and identity they will inevitably oppose some of yours – perhaps deliberately – but this is all part of a process of formulating and testing ideas and should not be seen as an affront. In advanced learning, defence of ideas using evidence is a key skill and so this is good practice.

Give them responsibility and don't worry if they make mistakes

Many parents find it difficult to know how much responsibility and freedom to give their children. In High Performance Learning we are trying to create students who are independent and autonomous, and so they need to have opportunities to develop this in low-risk situations and to practise it frequently. So while there is no blueprint for how to do this, the general principle is that independence in thought and action is useful. It is of course easier to achieve this with some children than others, hence gentle encouragement and a lot of patience are sometimes the order of the day.

Becoming independent in action and in thought is best achieved as an unleashing process. Too high expectations of autonomy can be unsettling for some children and they will need constant encouragement to try new things, for example, taking up new sports or joining clubs. They also need to know that they can give them up if they do not work out. Conversely, persisting beyond initial experience is also important. Often, learning new skills takes time and has some ups and downs. Becoming proficient in sport or in music takes practice and requires the ability to keep going when it is tough. Cognitive learning is just the same. Not always easy but eventually rewarding.

The most recent research shows that helping your child really can make a difference to academic performance, and that the strongest associations are found when families have high academic expectations for their children, develop and maintain communication with them about school activities, and help them to develop reading habits.

Enrichment providers

High Performance Learning recognises the importance of enrichment and sees it as having a prime position in the overall set of learning opportunities. It has a number of advantages. Enrichment activities expand on students' learning in ways that differ from the methods used during the school day. It can broaden horizons, develop new skills and contribute to students' personal and social development. Students benefit considerably from taking part in enrichment activities. These are often interactive and project-focused. They enhance a student's learning by bringing new concepts to light or by using old concepts in new ways. These activities are fun for the student, but they also impart knowledge. They often allow the participants to apply knowledge and skills developed in school to more practical and real-life experiences, as well as potentially ignite a passion or interest (see Figure 7.1).

Enrichment is not a new idea and many schools make good use of it. Indeed, my book (Eyre and Marjoram, 1990) was about precisely this issue. Schools offer enrichment activities themselves and also buy in provision from outside to enrich and enhance the student experience. We have a proud record of doing this and it can range from single activities and competitions through regular activities to intensive residential and summer schools.

Table 7.2 Top tips for parents

* Encourage curiosity – *Why do you think it is like that?*
* Imagination – *Let's pretend ...*
* Teach technique – *Try it like this ...*
* Use prompting questions – *What would happen if ...?*
* Introduce technical language – *The word for that is ...*
* Find a space to talk – *What did you learn at school today?*
* Encourage when things go wrong – *It takes 10,000 hours to make an expert ...*

... Listen, listen, listen ... Keep calm and don't give up!

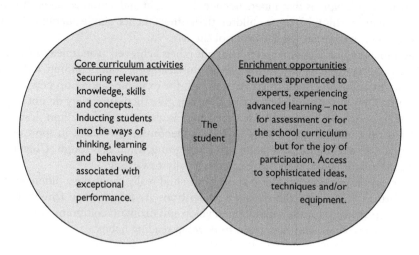

Core curriculum activities
Securing relevant
knowledge, skills
and concepts.
Inducting students
into the ways of
thinking, learning
and behaving
associated with
exceptional
performance.

The
student

Enrichment opportunities
Students apprenticed to
experts, experiencing
advanced learning – not
for assessment or for
the school curriculum
but for the joy of
participation. Access
to sophisticated ideas,
techniques and/or
equipment.

Figure 7.1 Developing enrichment opportunities

The topics are often designed to attract students and so may be on cryptography or garage bands as opposed to chemistry or music. They may also be cross-curricular and help students to see the links between subjects or domains. Some schools have off-timetable days or afternoons to make space for this freer form of learning and so give it recognition in the overall learning experiences. Enrichment activities can help students generate patterns for creative proficiency, build good character, initiate an engaged mode for learning, and find purpose in life.

Gifted education programmes have led to an explosion of enrichment opportunities for those identified as 'gifted' and are a regular part of the gifted education programme in many countries. They can serve either to supplement and enhance existing schooling or to compensate for it where challenge in the mainstream school is insufficient. Depending on their purpose, their detailed objectives for enrichment may be different but overall they share a common intention in making the most of time without syllabus or exam constraints. Being freed from the constraints of the core curriculum can allow students to dig deeper and explore more fully, or experience something new and broaden their horizons or experience a more advanced form of an activity than they do in school, e.g. algebra or drama.

However, enrichment is not restricted to these programmes but is an umbrella term used to describe learning in contexts as different as after-school clubs and university taster days. In short, it is a term used to describe experiences that fall outside core lesson time. The internet is full of great ideas for enrichment projects of all kinds and for all ages. Specialist subject communities have created banks of useful activities, and the theatre and the arts more widely have helped to provide good ideas for topics and activities.

Little is said about the pedagogy for enrichment activities; sometimes they can appear to be bolted onto learning in school and be entirely disconnected from it. This is not necessarily a bad thing. However, the impact of enrichment can be enhanced if it is recognised as being yet another opportunity for developing advanced skills and behaviours.

High Performance Learning can help enrichment providers to shape their work in a way that can amplify the core learning in school. Much enrichment is already stylistically enquiry-based and active, with students being asked to take risks, show independence and work collaboratively.

Enrichment is often delivered by experts and uses the novice-to-expert approach to developing greater expertise within the topic or subject. It may be developing specific domain skills or introducing ways of looking at materials, e.g. plants and seeds. It tends to be democratic in style and not assessed. NAGTY (2004) suggested that students should be permitted to be playful, precise and original and that this was best achieved by:

- the tutors working in an area in which they have a particular enthusiasm;
- a collegiate approach where everyone's views are considered of equal value;
- an enquiry-focused methodology requiring independent thinking within a structured setting;
- collaborative working opportunities to create maximum chance of originality;
- firm, fair, focused and constructive feedback to individuals to enable students to develop intellectually.

The High Performance Learning ACPs and VAAs can bring greater structure to enrichment activities and help to make enrichment activities more coherent in their aims. When used in High Performance Learning schools they can provide welcome opportunities for students to practise their development as well as linking enrichment to core schooling, not by content or style, but by the cognitive skills, values, attributes and attitudes being developed. Even when enrichment providers are not working with High Performance Learning schools, the High Performance Learning framework can assist with design and enhance the success of their activities. It can also provide a useful framework for evaluation of impact, which is a weak area for many enrichment programmes.

Universities

Levelling the playing field for students from disadvantaged backgrounds has been a topic of considerable focus in Europe and North America for many years. In the English context, the approaches have included a range of responses including bursaries, mentoring and outreach to schools. After 10 years of intensive activity the situation remains that, although there is a slight narrowing of the gap, students from the most advantaged areas are nearly ten times more likely to take up a place at a top university than those from the most disadvantaged areas. In January 2015, the English Higher Education Funding Council for England (HEFCE) announced a new £22 million scheme to encourage more young people into higher education. Some of the reasons why progress has been slow may be that students targeted for bursaries are unresponsive to financial inducements and place a high priority on provision that is local and socially comfortable

(Harrison and Hatt, 2012), or that these students do not aspire to the leading universities. But it is also because insufficient numbers of students from disadvantaged backgrounds obtain good exam scores and exhibit the 'college readiness' characteristics that universities so prize.

High Performance Learning is a practical mechanism for helping schools to create more students who can achieve highly in examinations and operate in ways that make them more college-ready. They should therefore be more compelling candidates at the time of entry. Students from disadvantaged backgrounds stand to benefit disproportionately from the High Performance Learning approach. By making explicit to these students the cognitive and behavioural skills that need to be developed and by providing them with regular and frequent quality opportunities to practise their development, this reduces dependency on cultural capital. In the past, some of these cognitive skills and values, attitudes and attributes have been transmitted at home and in particular in professional homes as a part of daily life, while students from disadvantaged backgrounds have not had similar levels of support. Schemes to assist in addressing this deficit have usually been short-term and of limited impact. They can and do raise aspirations, but they do little to secure advanced cognitive performance unless the teaching of these advanced skills is underpinning the pedagogy.

Universities could, however, do much to assist schools in embedding High Performance Learning theory and could use the same structures of ACPs and VAAs to underpin their outreach opportunities for students. This would serve to further reinforce their development by providing an expanded range of high-quality learning opportunities. What would be different would be that these additional opportunities would not be a bolt-on to core teaching, but rather another opportunity to practise and develop the core thinking and learning behaviours. This could help to give greater shape and continuity to university-led activities and help students to see how these fit with their wider schooling. All in all, by having a shared language with which to talk about advanced learning, schools and universities should be able to enhance their occasions for more insightful and meaningful interchanges.

Employers

High Performance Learning creates the kinds of students that employers have said they want to see. These are students who can think for themselves as well as having appropriate skills and attitudes for the workplace. When employers are working with schools or looking to develop stronger links, the High Performance Learning language can help to create better understanding and a smoother transition between the requirements of school, the university and the workplace. It can bring consensus to a sometimes polarised discussion.

In recruiting into the workplace, the progression grids for ACPs and VAAs can provide a useful tool for assessing strengths and weaknesses within individuals and identifying the support they will need if they are to continue to develop within the workplace. Success is a lifelong journey and the workplace has as much of a role to play in developing the cognitive skills and values, attitudes and attributes as the school or post-school study environment.

References

Coutinho, J. F., Silva, P. O. and Decety, J. (2014). Neurosciences, empathy, and healthy interpersonal relationships: Recent findings and implications for counseling psychology. *Journal of Counseling Psychology*, 61(4), 541–548. doi:10.1037/cou0000021.

Dweck, C. S. (2007). The perils and promises of praise. *Educational Leadership*, 65(2), 34–39.

Eyre, D. and Marjoram, T. (1990). *Enriching and Extending the National Curriculum*. London: Kogan Page.

Harrison, N. and Hatt, S. (2012). Expensive and failing? The role of student bursaries in widening participation and fair access in England. *Studies in Higher Education*, 37(6), 695–712. doi:10.1080/03075 079.2010.539679.

Kutner, L. (2013). How children develop empathy. *PsychCentral*. Available at: http://www.psychcentral.com/lib/how-children-develop-empathy/0001234 (accessed 19 May 2015).

NAGTY (2004). Unpublished guidance. Warwick: National Academy for Gifted and Talented Youth.

High Performance Learning

Becoming a world class school rubric

	1 Weak	2	3	4	5 Strong
1	Vision based on a profile of the type of student it wants to develop and accountability measures are built around this.	Teachers, students and parents are not able to articulate a student profile definition.				Teachers, students and parents can describe the kind of student the school produces and say why that is important.
2	A core curriculum that is overall well suited to the vision. Curriculum audited and then enhanced and supplemented where needed, including via the enrichment offer.	The school curriculum is: – that which has always been there; – externally set; – adopted wholesale from an external accreditation agency.				Teachers see the chosen curriculum as supporting the overall vision. It is deliberately supplemented to provide a broad and balanced range of opportunities that will develop the ACPs and VAAs. Numerous appropriate and well planned enrichment opportunities exist.
3	Students (and parents) are aware of what the school is trying to achieve and how they should participate.	Students and parents have a mostly passive role in the school, reacting and responding to the requests of teachers.				Students are active learners, confident and growing in autonomy. Schooling is done 'with' the student, not 'to' the student. Parents are active in support of their child's learning and work in harmony with the school.
4	The school is confident on behalf of its students. Students feel they can trust the school to help them be successful.	The teachers and senior team think educational outcomes are largely a result of inherited ability.				The teachers and senior team have high aspirations and expect *all* students to do well. They convey that confidence to students. There is a clear focus on removing barriers to achievement.
5	Personal and pastoral support and guidance are seen as crucial to academic success.	Teachers recognise that being safe and happy is important but do not connect that with academic achievement.				Everyone is aware that mental well-being and academic achievement are interlinked and the school has strong support generally and for individuals. Students feel that support.

(continued)

		1 Weak	2	3	4	5 Strong
6	The school is a well oiled machine that can deliver the same high standards for students year on year regardless of background.	Standards are good but vary year on year according to the strength of the cohort.				Standards in all year groups and year on year are universally high and improving annually. The school recognises that the success of students is its responsibility.
7	The school is purposeful but also relaxed, with students and staff equally at ease in the school.	The school is tense with control, the result of strict discipline.				The students and staff work to create a purposeful but relaxed environment in which all are respected and diversity is embraced.
8	There is a high level of trust in teachers, and their students and structures assume timely intervention and benchmarking rather than constant monitoring.	Monitoring structures are robust with teaching regularly reviewed by senior staff. Teachers produce good outcomes. Weak teachers are required to improve.				Teaching quality is consistently excellent. Teachers self-regulate and work collaboratively as part of a professional community to develop their practice. They are constantly seeking to improve. Most monitoring is peer to peer with occasional benchmarking from senior staff to ensure consistency of standards. Learning is frequently talked about in the school by students and teachers.
9	Internal accountability precedes external accountability and the school takes ownership for its own performance.	The school's own accountability structure is limited or is driven by external structures, e.g. inspection and changes significantly in line with external demands.				The school's own accountability structure is comprehensive and assesses all the elements needed to reach its vision. The school adheres to many external accountability frameworks, but expects to be largely compliant as a result of its accountability structures.
10	Everyone feels an emotional attachment to the school. However, the school does not see itself as world class because it is never complacent and is continually seeking to refine and improve.	Students, teachers and parents support the school.				Students, teachers and parents are proud to be involved with the school and keen to be ambassadors for it. Everyone thinks the school is great and everyone continues to put forward ideas for further improvements. The school welcomes these ideas.

High Performance Learning

Advanced Cognitive Performance
characteristics (ACPs)

META-THINKING	Meta-cognition	The ability to knowingly use a wide range of thinking approaches and to transfer knowledge from one circumstance to another.
	Self-regulation	The ability to monitor, evaluate and self-correct.
	Strategy planning	The ability to approach new learning experiences by actively attempting to connect them to existing knowledge or concepts and hence determine an appropriate way to *think* about the work.
	Intellectual confidence	The ability to articulate personal views based on evidence and where necessary defend them to others.
LINKING	Generalisation	The ability to see how what is happening in a particular instance could be extrapolated to other similar situations.
	Connection finding	The ability to use connections from past experiences to seek possible generalisations.
	'Big picture' thinking	The ability to work with big ideas and holistic concepts.
	Abstraction	The ability to move from concrete to abstract thought very quickly.
	Imagination	The ability to represent the problem and its categorisation in relation to more extensive and interconnected prior knowledge.
	Seeing alternative perspectives	The ability to take on the views of others and deal with complexity and ambiguity.
ANALYSING	Critical or logical thinking	The ability to deduct, hypothesise, reason and seek supporting evidence.
	Precision	The ability to work effectively within the rules of a domain.
	Complex and multi-step problem-solving	The ability to break down a task, decide on a suitable approach and then act.
CREATING	Intellectual playfulness	The ability to recognise rules and bend them to create valid but new forms.
	Flexible thinking	The ability to abandon one idea for a superior one or generate multiple solutions.
	Fluent thinking	The ability to generate ideas.
	Originality	The ability to conceive something entirely new.
	Evolutionary and revolutionary thinking	The ability to create new ideas through building on existing ideas or diverting from them.
REALISING	Automaticity	The ability to use some skills with such ease that they no longer require active thinking.
	Speed and accuracy	The ability to work at speed and with accuracy.

High Performance Learning

Progression in Advanced Cognitive Performance
characteristics

	Stage 2 Students:	Stage 4 Students:	Stage 6 Students:	Stage 8 Students:	Stage 10 Students:
Meta-cognition	• are aware of the thinking skills used to solve a problem	• are able to describe the thinking skills used to solve a problem	• are able to select appropriate thinking skills to solve a problem	• evaluate the range of possible approaches and select the most appropriate one(s) to improve efficiency	• use the full range of thinking skills fluently and comprehensively, including unconventionally
Self-regulation	• recognise that making errors is part of learning	• identify things that worked well and those that did not • begin to suggest goals for improvement	• are aware of own general strengths and weaknesses • make improvements to own practice and set future goals for improvement	• evaluate outcomes of changes and justify amendments/ improvements to the strategy	• make insightful observations and comments to continually refine and improve own personal best
Strategy planning	• recognise it is possible to consciously select an approach given to solve a problem	• are aware of the main approaches that could be deployed	• choose an appropriate approach to solve a problem or address an issue	• choose the most appropriate strategy and be able to justify the approach	• use strategy planning idependently as a way to solve problems or issues
Intellectual confidence	• begin to communicate own views based on experiences	• explain own views using examples and reasons	• present and justify own views using a diverse range of evidence	• evaluate the views of others and incorporate relevant evidence to construct and make persuasive arguments, including those they do not agree with	• synthesise a wide range of viewpoints and evidence to make a coherent and compelling personal argument

	Stage 2 Students:	Stage 4 Students:	Stage 6 Students:	Stage 8 Students:	Stage 10 Students:
Generalisation	• recognise simple patterns or similarities through observations	• use patterns, similarities and connections to make simple predictions	• identify and explain the connections between events, objects or ideas • develop generalisations • apply generalisations to an existing situation	• analyse similarities and differences between events, objects or ideas • develop generalisations, recognising complexity • apply generalisations to more complex situations	• understand the complexity of generalisations and apply these to a range of different situations with caution and justification
Connection finding	• be aware that different facts may be connected	• make simple and obvious connections, but do not grasp their significance	• make a number of connections, although miss the meta-connections and the significance for the whole • use prior knowledge to explain those links	• actively seek out connections when learning • transfer principles and ideas underlying one instance to another	• make connections not only within the given subject area, but also between and beyond subjects in inventive ways • make novel, insightful and innovative connections which help to reconceptualise
'Big picture' thinking	• begin to recognise that there are big ideas	• recognise there are big ideas and holistic concepts and begin to use them to make sense of things	• use big ideas and holistic concepts and make connections within and between them to make sense of experiences	• start new learning by focusing on big questions and/or locate new learning within a bigger picture	• explore the complexities and uncertainties in big ideas and holistic concepts and accept they have limitations

	Stage 2 Students:	Stage 4 Students:	Stage 6 Students:	Stage 8 Students:	Stage 10 Students:
Abstraction		• conduct processes in the head as opposed to using concrete materials	• take ideas, issues, problems or events and apply them to theoretical situations	• work with a range of ideas, issues, problems or events in order to explain abstract, theoretical situations or models	• evaluate a range of ideas, issues, problems or events, develop and combine them and apply them to complex imagined or theoretical situations
Imagination	• form plausible solutions to simple problems by asking 'what if ...?'	• envisage and create solutions in the mind to solve problems	• create novel solutions by drawing on prior knowledge	• picture solutions that are plausible but not common, linking together extensive prior knowledge	• explore alternative or new plausible solutions using extensive interconnected prior knowledge
Seeing alternative perspectives	• recognise that different people have different perspectives	• consider different interpretations or views and distinguish between facts, beliefs and opinions • are open to novelty	• weigh up the viewpoints of others, explain the influences that have shaped them, challenge or adopt different ideas appropriately	• critically evaluate the validity of viewpoints or arguments and objectively judge the evidence on which they are based, synthesising ideas where appropriate	• recognise that alternative viewpoints can be equally valid and be open to ambiguity • question assumptions

Linking

	Stage 2 Students:	Stage 4 Students:	Stage 6 Students:	Stage 8 Students:	Stage 10 Students:
Critical or logical thinking	• use information given to ask simple questions • begin to use information to explore ideas	• ask relevant questions and select and organise appropriate information from a range of sources to find answers and develop understanding • use selected information to explore ideas and make proposals	• identify questions and begin to refine them to clarify and deepen understanding • select and organise evidence to explore questions and test hypotheses • suggest answers based on evidence • process and manipulate evidence and assess it for validity	• prioritise questions to explore and develop relevant hypotheses • judge the reliability, validity and limitations of evidence • critically evaluate different sources of evidence • use evidence to challenge assumptions	• ask perceptive and insightful questions and develop relevant hypotheses • critically analyse and synthesise evidence and assess it for validity • use robust evidence to develop compelling new ideas and hypotheses
Precision	• begin to use simple symbols, conventions, vocabulary and language for the domain	• use simple symbols, conventions, vocabulary and language for the domain with some errors and omissions	• use skills and symbols, conventions, vocabulary for the domain with few errors and omissions	• use advanced skills symbols, conventions, vocabulary effectively to reach strong outcomes	• select appropriate skills and conventions and use effectively to reach strong outcomes
Complex and multi-step problem-solving	• use a given approach to solve simple problems, ideas or tasks	• are aware that complex tasks can be broken down and understand the techniques for achieving this	• select and use appropriate methodologies to solve more complex problems, explore more complex ideas or complete more complex tasks	• evaluate the effectiveness of different approaches and identify a preferred personal repertoire	• use a broad range of approaches effectively, selecting those most appropriate for particular problems

Analysing

	Stage 2 Students:	Stage 4 Students:	Stage 6 Students:	Stage 8 Students:	Stage 10 Students:
Intellectual playfulness	• are aware that there are rules in different domains and ask 'what if ...?'	• recognise the rules and conventions of different domains and choose some rules to disregard or change	• understand the complex rules and conventions of different domains and choose some rules to modify, recognising some of the consequences	• imaginatively adapt and bend the rules of a domain for a specific purpose, outcome or consequence	• use the rules flexibly, bending them where appropriate to create novel, fun or interesting outcomes
Flexible thinking	• be aware there are often different solutions to a problem	• be willing to abandon one idea in favour of another on the basis of reason and evidence	• adopt new ideas easily in response to convincing reason and evidence and recognise some consequences	• expect to look beyond first ideas and seek others in order to select a best fit	• routinely think beyond the accepted approach and consider multiple ideas so as to create best-fit solutions
Fluent thinking	• brainstorm ideas, with help, in response to simple problems	• independently generate multiple solutions and ideas in response to more complex problems	• frequently propose to others solutions resulting from brainstorming ideas for complex problems, evidence or issues	• routinely seek to explore a wide range of possibilities before posing a solution to complex problems, evidence or issues	• create compelling ideas which demonstrate originality

Creating

Originality	• create a slight variation to accepted ideas	• create several new ideas to address a problem, seeing possibilities others have not seen	• create a range of new and unique modifications to address a problem or create an item	• create and model a range of new and unique ideas to address a problem, recognising practical implications and conflicting demands	• insightfully create and model innovative and unique ideas and evaluate them
Evolutionary and revolutionary thinking	• create a new idea by building on existing ideas or diverting from them	• create several new ideas to address a problem by building on existing ideas or diverting from them	• create a range of new ideas to address a problem, recognising limitiations and suggesting solutions by building on existing ideas or diverting from them • choose a completely different way to address the task	• create and model a range of new ideas to address a task, recognising practical implications and conflicting demands by building on existing ideas or diverting from them	• create and model innovative ideas – both evolutionary and revolutionary, and evaluate them by building on existing ideas or diverging from them

	Stage 2 Students:	Stage 4 Students:	Stage 6 Students:	Stage 8 Students:	Stage 10 Students:
Automaticity	• recall simple key facts, concepts and ideas relevant to the stage of learning with some support	• recall more complex key facts, concepts and ideas relevant to the stage of learning and with increased independence • show fluency in basic age-related tasks so they can be done without thinking, e.g. times tables	• independently recall complex key facts, concepts and ideas relevant to the stage of learning • exhibit fluency in an increasing range of key skills	• easily recall advanced key facts, concepts and ideas relevant to the stage of learning • acquire new rules and use them fluently	• effortlessly use key facts, concepts and ideas relevant to the stage of learning • draw upon a range of skills without the need to think or process
Speed and accuracy	• begin to develop relevant skills and use with some accuracy	• use relevant skills with increasing accuracy • mostly work to the speed required for the task	• actively seek accuracy in work and understand its importance • consistently complete work on time	• achieve good levels of accuracy in work • plan work and pace speed needed to complete it – even with multi-step tasks	• strive for and achieve excellent levels of accuracy in work • work rapidly without errors

Realising

High Performance Learning
Values, Attitudes and Attributes (VAAs)

EMPATHETIC	Collaborative	The ability to seek out opportunities to receive responses to your work; to present your own views and ideas clearly and concisely; to listen to the views of others; be willing and able to work in teams; to assume a variety of roles and be able to evaluate your own ideas and contributions.
	Concerned for society	The ability to know the contribution you can make to society to the benefit of those less fortunate; to demonstrate citizenship and a sense of community ethos and recognise differences as well as similarities between people and peoples; be aware of your own and others' cultural heritage and be sensitive to the ethical and moral issues raised by your studies.
	Confident	The ability to develop a belief in your knowledge, understanding and action; recognise when you need to change your beliefs based upon additional information or the arguments of others; deal with new challenges and situations, including when this places you under stress.
AGILE	Enquiring	The ability to be curious; be willing to work alone; be proactive; keen to learn; show enterprise and independent thought; challenge assumptions and require evidence for assertions; actively control your own learning; move on from the absorption of knowledge and procedures to developing your own views and solutions.
	Creative and enterprising	The ability to be open-minded and flexible in your thought processes; demonstrate a willingness to innovate and invent new and multiple solutions to a problem or situation; adapt your approach according to need; surprise and show originality in your work, so developing a personal style; be resourceful when presented with challenging tasks and problems, using your initiative to find solutions.
	Open-minded	The ability to take an objective view of different ideas and beliefs; become more receptive to other ideas and beliefs based on the arguments of others; change ideas, should there be compelling evidence to do so.
	Risk-taking	The ability to demonstrate confidence; experiment with novel ideas and effects; speculate willingly; work in unfamiliar contexts; avoid coming to premature conclusions; tolerate uncertainty.
HARD-WORKING	Practice	The ability to train and prepare through repetition of the same processes in order to become more proficient.
	Perseverance	The ability to keep going and not give up; encounter obstacles and difficulties but never give up; persist in effort; work diligently and work systematically; do not be satisfied until high quality, appropriate precision and the desired outcome are achieved.
	Resilience	The ability to overcome setbacks; remain confident, focused, flexible and optimistic; help others to move forward in the face of adversity.

High Performance Learning

Progression in Values, Attitudes and
Attributes

		Stage 2 Students:	Stage 4 Students:	Stage 6 Students:	Stage 8 Students:	Stage 10 Students:
EMPATHETIC	Collaborative	• talk in small groups and pairs about themselves • listen to others in pairs and small groups and present and share their ideas • demonstrate their listening skills by asking the speaker questions	• clearly articulate their own ideas to the group • listen to the ideas of others and reinterpret these ideas in their own words using positive language • begin to take on board suggestions from others in the group	• present confidently to other groups in the class and classes further down the school about their work • recognise the role of others in development of ideas and start modelling the skills of collaboration to younger students • see and explain the advantages of collaborating	• tailor their presentation to meet the needs of their audience • see the value of adapting their views and ideas to resolve issues, achieve shared goals and outcomes and help the group progress • are aware that in different situations they need to take on different roles to develop or build on the strengths of others and get the job done	• present to groups outside of the familiar and outside of the school • develop others in the group as collaborators by putting them in new and unfamiliar situations and not just playing on their strengths • know to whom to assign different roles in order to complete a task based on others' strengths and experience

		Stage 2 Students:	Stage 4 Students:	Stage 6 Students:	Stage 8 Students:	Stage 10 Students:
EMPATHETIC	Concerned for society	• recognise the difference between right and wrong • develop an awareness of who others are in the school and local community and have an opinion about change	• seek to help others in the class, school and local community and willingly participate in group activities to tackle issues • have a sense of justice and rationalise why change is needed in simple terms • identify projects in the community and suggest possible options to complete them	• willingly participate in the community (both local and global), identifying needs and courses of action to meet those needs • comfortably work with others to meet those needs • begin to have an understanding of human rights • develop a stronger sense of justice, drawing on international events	• develop critical opinions on global issues and comfortably debate these using evidence • adjust personal behaviour to fit belief systems and have a strong sense of their place in the world • understand the relationship between the rights of the individual and the laws of society • appreciate the benefits of a diverse society	• take proactive and direct action to help in the wider community • analyse how different circumstances, belief systems and emotions influence events and act independently according to their own belief systems • proactively initiate issue-based campaigns • challenge injustice and take the needs of present and future generations into account
AGILE	Confident	• realise there are things they know and understand and things they do not • with help, admit their mistakes and learn from them	• articulate their knowledge, understanding and ideas • listen to the ideas and opinions of others	• believe in their knowledge, understanding and ideas • enjoy discussing their beliefs, ideas or behaviours with others • deal with new challenges and situations	• justify their beliefs, ideas or behaviours • realise when they may need to change beliefs, ideas or behaviours based on new information or the arguments of others • enjoy new challenges and situations	• critically reflect on their knowledge, understanding and ideas in the light of new experiences and interaction with others • know when to modify their knowledge, understanding and ideas based on their critical reflection • seek new challenges and situations

AGILE		Stage 2 Students:	Stage 4 Students:	Stage 6 Students:	Stage 8 Students:	Stage 10 Students:
	Enquiring	• begin to develop their natural curiosity • identify, with guidance, questions and problems which interest them • plan to undertake research with guidance and collect, store and organise information relevant to the research	• identify questions and problems and justify their interest in them • plan and carry out research unaided, and collect relevant information • identify the strengths and weaknesses of information and whether it is relevant to their enquiry, with guidance • consider different viewpoints on issues, events or problems	• identify appropriate research steps and strategies, and begin to refine and modify methods of inquiry • realise which information is useful and relevant and communicate analysis in an appropriate way • consider why there are different viewpoints, and begin to make connections between them • challenge assumptions and make evidence-based assertions	• explain their research techniques to others, describing and justifying the methods they have chosen • begin to teach others the skills of enquiry • make informed and well reasoned decisions and require evidence for others' assertions	• independently identify questions and problems, justify their interest in them, and critically consider whether they are worth asking and solving • use connections from across the curriculum to develop their enquiry, answering questions that are of real value to society both in school and outside
	Creative and enterprising	• explore different solutions to problems that are set for them • are interested in the world around them • produce pieces of work that are original to them in form or content	• ask questions about their own learning and seek ways of finding their own answers • create original work that demonstrates good outcomes in terms of quality and suitability for the task set	• experiment with unfamiliar approaches or forms and decide on the right ones for the right circumstances • develop a sense of their own personal style in the work they create	• choose increasingly innovative approaches to solving problems and creating work • are able to adapt to a wide variety of purposes and audiences without sacrificing quality	• provide original and elegant solutions to complex problems • create novel and surprising pieces of work of high quality and that are fit for purpose

		Stage 2 Students:	Stage 4 Students:	Stage 6 Students:	Stage 8 Students:	Stage 10 Students:
AGILE	Open-minded	• are becoming aware that other people may have different ideas and beliefs and come from different backgrounds	• recognise that other people may have different ideas and beliefs and are prepared to listen to them • may change their mind based on the ideas and beliefs of others • show an interest in people from other cultures and backgrounds	• can take an objective view of different ideas and beliefs • become more receptive to different ideas and beliefs based on the argument of others • will change their ideas should there be compelling evidence to do so • appreciate the benefit of knowing, and working with, people from other cultures	• evaluate new information or the arguments of others and are willing to change beliefs, ideas or behaviours based on their evaluation • evaluate cultural perspectives by drawing on the views of people from other cultures and backgrounds when forming opinions	• seek out new information and the arguments of others in order to reflect critically on their knowledge, understanding and ideas and modify them on the basis of their critical reflection • systematically take a considered global stance when approaching new ideas
	Risk-taking	• realise that things we do involve an element of risk-taking • talk about known risks in everyday situations and ways to approach those risks if they affect personal safety and well-being	• weigh up positive and negative risks in new situations and suggest different solutions and approaches to those situations based on their assessment • confidently approach new and unknown situations, seeing them as a challenge to be faced	• try out new ideas in different situations, drawing on previous experience • speculate on the outcomes of taking certain risks in unfamiliar situations	• recognise that we cannot always predict the outcome of a situation – that some things in life are unknown • approach unfamiliar situations positively, and with confidence and acceptance of the unknown	• speculate and take risks in a whole variety of situations, known and unknown • assess situations in terms of personal safety and well-being • confidently tackle new challenges and make different decisions based on understanding of previous decisions and mistakes

		Stage 2 Students:	Stage 4 Students:	Stage 6 Students:	Stage 8 Students:	Stage 10 Students:
	Practice	• repeat work in order to improve	• practise regularly in order to improve • understand the value of practice in improving performance • respond to feedback from others about next steps to improvement and how to improve	• establish and follow practice schedules • seek and respond to feedback on how to improve performance • respond to goals set by others for improvements	• take responsibility for practising independently and regularly • jointly set goals for improvements • monitor own performance and seek feedback from others	• self-regulate and revise practice schedules in line with improvements • set own goals and monitor progress towards them • actively seek out ways to improve
HARD-WORKING	Perseverance	• work for extended periods of time on a task with encouragement • recognise that there may be obstacles to their progress	• work for sustained periods of time and can see the benefits of doing so • identify distractions and begin to recognise the effect these might have on their work	• are self-motivated to work on extended projects • identify distractions and manage them to minimise their effect • see the long-term benefits of performing a task to completion	• independently plan an activity or project beyond what is asked of them • identify and use strategies for setting and meeting personal targets in order to increase personal motivation	• recognise and accept that making mistakes is a natural part of learning, and can explain this to others • have enough self-awareness and confidence to accept that some tasks cannot be completed

		Stage 2 Students:	Stage 4 Students:	Stage 6 Students:	Stage 8 Students:	Stage 10 Students:
HARD-WORKING	Resilience	• complete tasks with support, recognising some frustrations	• learn ways to manage their own time and work towards personal targets they have set • complete longer tasks with increasing independence, recognising frustrations that inhibit performance	• show greater independence in setting personal goals and targets • use time effectively and persist with extended tasks to completion, recognising strategies, overcoming frustration and distractions and seeing the long-term benefits	• self-manage extended and complex tasks to completion • employ appropriate strategies to complete tasks and consistently overcome frustrations and barriers	• select and self-manage extended and complex tasks consistently to completion • are deliberately unwilling to allow adversity to prevent them from reaching their goal and are unswerving in their focus on their eventual success

Index